Cash Crops
for the Thrifty Gardener

Cash Crops
for the
Thrifty Gardener

Geri Harrington

A GD/Perigee Book

Perigee Books
are published by
The Putnam Publishing Group
200 Madison Avenue
New York, New York 10016

Designed by Lee Ann Chearneyi

Library of Congress Cataloging in Publication Data

Harrington, Geri.
Cash crops for the thrifty gardener.

Includes index.
1. Horticulture.   2. Gardening.   I. Title.
SB318.H34   1983   635   83-8315
ISBN 0-399-50752-3

First printing, 1983

Printed in the United States of America
1 2 3 4 5 6 7 8 9 10

Contents

6 Cash Crops for the Thrifty Gardener

Introduction

Today prices are rising rapidly in the produce market and quality is dropping as fruits and vegetables are developed for their ability to stand up under modern distribution methods rather than for their flavor and texture. As a result, home gardeners are coming to depend more and more on their own gardens as a source of reasonably priced, high-quality produce. While there is no doubt that home-grown produce is tastier and fresher, it is not invariably less expensive. When your garden is bursting with zucchini, super-market zucchini is selling for pennies a pound, and potatoes at ten pounds for 69 cents are not a cost-effective crop for the small home garden.

There is, however, a way not only to cut the cost of gardening but actually to realize a cash return from your crops without depriving yourself of the pleasure of your own garden-fresh tomato or a roomful of your own cut flowers. Growing cash crops is mostly a matter of planning. Whether your garden is large or small, in city or country, mainly vegetables or all flowers, you can grow enough to sell without depriving yourself of the fruits of your labor.

The best thing about planning for cash crops is that you can make a garden to suit yourself and your needs. Your garden plan is completely flexible: it can change from year to year, profit from mistakes you may make, or be adapted to make the most of what you learn from experience. Best of all, you are in complete control and can do whatever you please.

There are three basic rules for growing cash crops:

1. Cut gardening costs as much as possible so as to increase your profit margin.

2. Plan your garden, giving maximum space to cash-producing crops.

3. Develop your markets so you can sell your crops for the best prices.

Costs can be cut in a number of ways. If you think of your labor as a cost, gardening more efficiently—for example, mulching to cut down on watering or intensive gardening to reduce weeds—is the first step. The city gardener who gardens on a terrace or in a small backyard garden may already be practicing these labor-saving methods; the country gardener, with more space in which to work, may have fallen into inefficient habits but should welcome the change.

The next area to look for savings is in fertilizer and mulch. A compost heap is not only organically and environmentally sound but also turns kitchen waste into first-class fertilizer. City gardeners often think they cannot have a compost heap, but this is not so. Compost heaps can be built in all sorts of containers, including large wooden crates and plastic garbage cans. If you are not handy, containers specially designed for this purpose can be bought at garden centers or purchased through seed catalogs.

Planning for cash crops is the next step, and this is fun. When you go through the seed catalog to make up your order, notice the items that you know are luxuries. Among vegetables, for instance, shallots, Jerusalem artichokes, and Belgian endive are always expensive even at the peak of their seasons. And almost any cut flowers you grow to sell will bring a good price. Of course, you won't want to give over the entire garden to cash crops—you may still want to grow zucchini—but you can start with a small patch of something easy and prolific, like shallots or lilies of the valley. The important thing is to start thinking of your garden plan in terms of some produce to sell. Shallots, for instance, will save in two ways: they will bring in cash and they will save you the out-of-pocket expense of buying them for your own use.

The last step in cash-cropping is developing your markets. Look around you—the nearer the better—and find a place (or places) to sell what you grow. Perhaps the markets you now shop at, perhaps the health-food store you keep meaning to visit. Perhaps the florist who always tempts you over your budget. Any place that sells produce or flowers is a potential market for your cash crops. If you feel you can't do this because you don't know how to sell anything, don't worry: I'll tell you exactly how to go about it in a later chapter.

Start small and start now. Here in one book is everything you need to know: how to plan a cash-crop garden, suggestions on what to grow, what records to keep, how to price your produce, and how to package and sell for the retail market.

Good luck! And may your garden grow dollars as well as dahlias.

Getting
Started

1. Planning the Garden

If you live in the country or in a suburb, chances are that you already have a garden. It may consist of shrubbery around the house—foundation planting—plus maybe a flower bed or two, with tulips in the spring and annuals blooming through the summer. The very shady spot in one area may already be green with pachysandra, and you may have a few rose bushes for garden and cut flowers. It is hard to imagine, however, that you do not also grow some vegetables—at least several tomato plants—in a small corner plot in full sun. You may also have a larger plot with radishes, green beans, and zucchini. Some gardeners who have only a small area available will devote the entire space to corn; others will have to have at least a few peppers. This is all determined by personal preference or whim and with no expectation of the land earning its keep. What I am suggesting is a more calculated use of space to bring both personal and culinary pleasure and to augment your income. This will require planning your garden with an entirely different frame of reference.

If your goal is merely beautiful grounds, you can proceed quite differently from the gardener who wishes a crop from the vegetable and flower garden. For the former you can engage the services of a landscape gardener or get advice from the local nurseryman. If you make a mistake, the bulbs can always be moved and the annuals chosen differently the following year until you find combinations that are pleasing and enhance your house and grounds. Only the choices of placement for large items, such as specimen trees, should be considered comparatively permanent decisions; most of your plantings can be altered from year to year until, through trial and error, your grounds achieve a finished look.

A vegetable and flower cash crop—though still decorative—is a totally different proposition. The aim here is yield, and each season's crop lays your expertise and planning on the line. A poor crop any given year is perceived as a failure. Though it may not be your fault, and your living, thank heaven, does not depend on it, you will still feel that perhaps it could have been prevented by better management. While there is no way of achieving success every season with every crop, the best method of preventing failures and the surest way to more successes than failures is to put more thought into the work that should be done before you ever touch spade to soil.

Siting the Garden

If you are fortunate enough to have the space, you can site your garden perfectly. Simply pick a spot that receives full sun eight hours a day, on a slight slope toward the south, away from any sizable stand of trees or tree roots, near your outdoor water outlet, handy to your kitchen door, and not over your well or septic field (if your home is in a really rural area).

If you can fill all of the above requirements, you can manage with only six hours of sun a day; eight, however, is better. If you cannot fill all of those requirements, remember that the one that is absolutely essential is the sun. It is true that some vegetables, like lettuce, will tolerate a little more shade, especially in the heat of summer, but it is best to assume that this is not the case. If you do not have a reasonably sunny spot anywhere on your grounds, you cannot grow vegetables. (You might still be able to manage cherry tomatoes and some other amenable vegetables in a sunny window.)

After sun, the next most important factor is soil, which I will talk about in the next chapter.

Next, survey your site for its proximity to trees. Tree root networks are larger than you can possibly imagine, and they go deep into the ground as well as spreading horizontally near the surface. As a rule of thumb, assume the tree roots extend to the circumference of the tree as measured by its extending branches. This will not be true for some species of trees, such as black locusts, but these will advertise their greater spread by growing close to or slightly above the soil surface; in spading the garden area you will soon be aware of this type of root. No vegetable plant can compete for soil nutrients with the appetite of a tree root; you will find it impossible to furnish enough nutrients for both the tree and the vegetable. In addition, tree roots make it difficult to rototill the garden and to grow root vegetables that are not misshapen and weak. Even a pretty dogwood or crabapple tree outside your vegetable garden may cause problems in the corner nearest to it.

Stands of trees (as compared to one or two specimen plantings) present another problem. Air flows like water. During chilly spells or during the winter months, cold air will flow along the tops of the trees and drop to the ground when it reaches the end of the grove. If your vegetable garden happens to be at the end of this stand of trees, the area will be much colder than the rest of your grounds. This additional cold can be just enough to cause an earlier frost in your garden than in any other part of your property.

Convenience is another important point in siting a vegetable garden. If you can dash out for a green pepper for your salad or a snip of chives or an extra zucchini, you will find yourself using much more of your crop. Otherwise, since we are usually making meals in the middle or at the end of a busy day, you may skip that extra ingredient rather than take the trouble to go all the way out to the vegetable garden to pick it. Another plus for convenience is that it is much easier to keep an eye on your garden when you pass it often or can look out on it from a window. You are more likely to notice an early infestation of pests or the fact that a baby woodchuck has discovered your broccoli. And if your site is in a family high-traffic area, the rabbits, the woodchucks, and the neighbor's dog will be less likely to linger.

Convenience also includes being near a water source. Vegetable gardens cannot be dependent on nature for water: she is too capricious. A dry spell will require a great deal of judicious watering to keep your crops growing without interruption, and watering can become a very wearing, time-consuming, and tedious chore if you have to drag a long, heavy hose any considerable distance.

How to Decide Between Vegetables and Flowers

Until fairly recently many people had never grown vegetables. They may have been avid flower gardeners, but they preferred to buy their food, and, perhaps, thought growing it was not very glamorous. Raising the perfect rose has always had more cachet than raising the perfect turnip.

The new interest in nutrition, as well as the high prices of vegetables, has brought about a considerable change. At a dollar a head, lettuce has become a much more interesting crop to the home gardener. And many people have reacted so strongly against the plastic tomato—the only variety usually to be found at the supermarket—that they eat canned tomatoes throughout most of the year until the local farmers' markets have native produce.

For most gardeners, therefore, the choice has not been between flowers and vegetables but among the many vegetables they can choose to grow. And many have learned to increase the number of vegetables by selecting some that are beautiful enough to be included in the flower bed. I grow snow peas, for instance, at the back of one of my narrow flower beds in front of the house. The delicate lavender or white blossoms, with their lovely light-green foliage, are as decorative as sweet peas. By the end of June the vines can be pulled up and annual flowers put in to cover up the empty space. In front of the same bed I grow successive crops of lettuce, which I use as a bedding plant as well as a salad green. A row of miniature bibb lettuces is pretty and very neat and self-contained. Salad-bowl lettuce makes a taller, bushier, but very attractive border. If I gather it leaf by leaf, instead of taking a whole plant, I can extend its decorative usefulness. When all of it is eventually eaten, I can either take out a plant at a time, replacing it with any number of small bedding flowering plants, or remove the whole row and replace it. Seeds of either lettuce or flowering annuals can be sown near the mature plants and will soon fill in the bed, slightly farther back from the original planting, with attractive seedlings. Or the whole head can be picked and replaced with a plant or seedling, and the transition will be practically complete as soon as you have harvested the last head.

Many vegetables have especially attractive flowers; the rose-scented Chinese chive has starry white flowers, the common chive has beautiful lavender balls (good to eat, incidentally), and squash blossoms are both beautiful and edible. Of course many flower blossoms are also edible. And if you have never made use of the peppery buds of nasturtiums, you are in for a new taste treat.

Choosing Your Vegetables

Although we are going to talk about gardening for profit, we are not doing so at the expense of your pleasure in gardening or your own taste buds, so the first thought in choosing your vegetables is to consult your own personal preferences. In other words, what do you like to eat?

Make a list of your favorite vegetables; look them up in a standard garden book, or ask your cooperative extension service for a hardiness zone map, or go to the store and look on the back of seed packets, to find out whether you can grow them in your area. Some vegetables need a long growing season and will do well in the South but not in New England, which has a shorter summer. Some like cold weather and will be fine from Philadelphia north but hard to grow in Georgia, where it gets too hot. Even in New England you would not plant snow peas in the summer, because they prefer the cooler temperatures of spring and fall. On the other hand, tomatoes need warm temperatures of at least 65 degrees Fahrenheit, so you cannot start them in the ground in March (though you may have noticed that self-sown seeds—left in the ground from the previous summer—will sprout once the ground reaches that temperature). An easy way to choose from a list of vegetables that will grow in your area is to get a seed catalog from a seedsman in your part of the country. For instance, Nichols in Oregon, Johnny's Selected Seeds from Maine, and Park in South Carolina all feature field-grown crops.

Before you finish planning your garden, read the marketing section of this book. You may be very fond of onions but may decide to grow shallots instead and buy onions. The same with vegetable spaghetti vs zucchini. As a general rule, substitute an expensive-to-buy version of what you like to eat for the inexpensive, more common vegetable that will be selling for pennies in the market just when your own crop is ripening. (More on this in Chapter 3.)

Plotting the Garden

The next step in choosing your vegetables is to draw a scale plan of your garden. The lines don't have to be ruler-straight (although with graph paper that is easy), but the area should be accurately measured. Scale your plot like a map—ten feet to the inch, for instance—so that you can plan accurately. Then make a list of your vegetables and write down how far apart the mature plants must stand and how far apart the rows should be.

Tip:

You can save space by growing vegetables up instead of letting them sprawl on the ground. You would naturally give snow peas and pole beans something to grow on, but you might never think of growing vegetable spaghetti up a fence. Cucumbers also do well vertically, and so do many other vegetables that would otherwise take up a great deal of ground space if left to their druthers.

Now take your favorite vegetables and decide where in your garden to put them. Be sure to put low-growing vegetables in front of taller vegetables so that both get the sun. Figure out how much space the number of plants you want will take (or, if you are limited, how many plants you can fit into the space you have), and mark that off on your plan, labeling the section for a vegetable and making little circles for each plant.

Work down your list from favorite to next favorite, until you have used up all the space in your garden. Now see what remains on the list. If you are short of space, with many more vegetables you would like to include, take another look. Maybe you are planting too many radishes at one time. Radishes are best picked when ready, and most families do not eat enormous quantities of them. Since they grow very quickly, it is best to plan successive plantings. An easy way to do this is to fertilize every so often. Then every time you pick a radish, drop a bead of fertilizer in the hole, fill to planting level, and plant another seed. That way you will have a steady crop without taking up a lot of space. You can do the same thing with carrots and beets; pick the first crop really young so that you have plenty of time for a second crop.

Sometimes you can actually plant two vegetables in the same space at the same time. For instance, radish seeds are often planted along with carrot seeds; the former sprout quickly and make it easier for the slower sprouting carrot seedlings to reach the soil surface. The radishes mature and are eaten while the carrots are just beginning to form. So you can have your radishes and carrots too! Another example is corn and pole beans. The pole beans need something to grow on, and corn is ideal. After you have harvested the corn you will have pole beans maturing on the dead stalks. Lettuce can be planted among broccoli plants and will mature long before the broccoli plants create too much shade.

Once you have made these adjustments to your original plan, take another look. If you have combined perennials with annuals, it won't work. Perennials should be put in a part of the garden that can go undisturbed by the Rototiller year after year, without making it too difficult to turn over the rest of the garden. Asparagus and rhubarb, for instance, should last for years once they have become established; they should have their own undisturbed area. One solution would be to put them in a perennial flower bed; the asparagus foliage is attractive and the crimson stalks and dark-green crinkled leaves of the rhubarb are definitely decorative. On the other hand, both these vegetables are very heavy feeders, and asparagus spreads considerably from its original planting.

Some vegetables are almost unfit for the regular vegetable garden and should really have places of their own. Jerusalem artichokes are harmful to anything growing near them and spread alarmingly if put in the regular garden. Horseradish is also a rapid and spreading grower and is best put, along with peppermint, where it can be confined without difficulty.

If the vegetables you are thinking of including are discussed specifically in this book, check out their sections to make sure there are not other factors to consider. And remember not to try to grow vegetables among acid-loving shrubbery or plants, for the soil that is good for one will be unsatisfactory for the other.

Do not try to cheat on space. If you want to grow melons or winter squash, you will fool only yourself by trying to squeeze them into a small area (although, as I have mentioned, you may be able to grow some of them vertically by supporting the fruit when it gets heavy).

If you garden the intensive way, you can produce a heavier crop than if you stick to conventional row planting. I plant radishes by sowing them almost scatter fashion—never in rows—in a very small plot. When they mature, they are practically touching one another. It doesn't seem to bother them a bit to be crowded. Carrots also take well to this method and so do beets. Foliage plants, such as lettuce and broccoli, can usually be set much closer together than recommended without any loss of yield. Planting all of these vegetables more closely means that the ground will be completely shaded by the plants, and you will find that weeding is much less of a problem than when you leave so much ground exposed. Since I discovered intensive planting, I plant very few things in rows (leeks are an exception because they grow in a trench) and thus save the time I used to spend trying to get my rows straight.

If you have a choice, choose vegetables that are disease-resistant. Most of the time the packet or seed catalog will give you this information. This is more important with certain vegetables than with others, but you will avoid the temptation to use pesticides and insecticides if you choose varieties that can take care of themselves. Of course you will still run into problems; but if you do not expect to avoid them, you won't panic no matter what happens.

In choosing vegetables, also consider the number of days to maturity. You may want to plan your sales so that you have some income coming in all summer; this will mean planting some fast-maturing crops as well as those that will come in later on. Scallions, for instance, will give quick results. Be sure, also, you have enough time between planting and the first frost date in your area. You may settle for half-grown vegetables, but unless they are the kind that command premium prices—like baby beets and garden peas—you will short-change yourself in the market. If you want to grow something for which you do not have a long enough outdoor season, you can extend it by about six weeks by starting the seeds indoors. This is easy to do with many flowers and vegetables, but you need very specific growing conditions—such as enough artificial light— and a large enough space to make it worthwhile. I usually do it with flowers—especially those that are expensive to buy, such as lupines—but rarely with vegetables. The worst problem with an early indoor start is a white-fly infestation. A neighbor of mine lost sixty tomato plants he had lovingly raised for weeks and weeks to that tenacious pest. Damping off of young seedlings is another problem, although that is fairly easily controlled by using sterilized soil and well washed tools and containers, or peat pots.

Never leave your garden bare during the growing season. Once you have harvested a crop, dispose of it to make room for a new planting. Always remember to refertilize and to dig up the area again if it has become less fluffy and easy to work. I must admit I often fail to do this, and plants that are no longer producing stand reproachfully waiting for replacements. But you are trying to produce cash crops, so it is important to keep the garden producing at all times.

Try to rotate crops so that you do not plant the same vegetable too often in the same spot. I generally stick to one area during a growing season to simplify my planning (unless I have allowed for spring and midsummer plans in the first place), but the next year I move everything around wherever possible. My one exception to this has been tomatoes because in my small garden there is just one really ideal site for tomatoes; I must confess I have been putting them there for twenty years. So far I have not had any problems, but I am extra careful in fertilizing that site and dig in a great deal of manure and compost each season. This is definitely not good garden practice since, theoretically, tomatoes should never be grown in the same spot in two consecutive seasons. I think I have been lucky, and each summer I expect to run into trouble; so far I have nòt. I am extra careful in cleaning up the garden before winter so that no debris is left to winter over and provide a home and safe harbor for diseases and pests. Also, if I have time, I turn over the surface of the soil to expose any harmful insects to winter frosts.

When making your garden plan, be sure to allow room for yourself. If you have to tiptoe between your plots to cultivate, weed, or harvest, you won't enjoy gardening. Leave enough of a path to bring your wheelbarrow to at least the center of the garden. And be sure each plot is small enough so that you can reach into the center of it from your footpath.

Seeds

You will want to send for several catalogs (see Appendix B for list) for as wide as possible a selection of seeds, varieties and prices. Some day when I get well organized I want to buy a seed packet at the local garden shop and also order the same seeds from several seedsmen. That is the only way I will know whether I am really shopping wisely. I have been told that seed packages bought off the rack do not contain as many seeds for the money as the same seeds ordered from a seed catalog. I have never tested this theory, although I really should, now that seeds have become so very expensive.

One clear advantage to ordering from a seed catalog is that you have a much wider choice. Store racks cannot possibly offer the selection found in a catalog and tend to be stocked with only the most popular types and varieties of plants; a seed catalog can do much better. Instead of one or two varieties of cucumbers, a seed catalog may offer ten. If you are at all adventurous, this will be irresistible. If you are going in for cash crops, you will definitely want to try a few new vegetables each season.

I have found that certain brands of seeds carried on the racks are definitely inferior and have a lower germination rate. Beware of bargains that may not be bargains; the only way to know for sure is to try a few and see how they work out. Buy one packet of something that germinates quickly, such as radishes, and you will still have time to go back and buy additional packets if the radishes work out. Keeping a simple journal of your garden is one way to put all this information at your fingertips for next year.

Do not be tempted by "new" on seed packets or in catalogs; it invariably means that the seeds for that particular item will be more expensive than tried-and-true varieties. You can wait until it has been around awhile and has come down to a more sensible price. Whether you are buying roses or green beans, the varieties that have just been developed will be offered at premium prices for no better reason than that they are new. You may think you can get a higher price in the market for new varieties or that it will enhance your image as a gardener to offer the latest creation, but the higher price is problematical. Beans are beans, and few customers will pay much more for a new variety, especially if the difference is not obvious. Sometimes, also, a new vegetable takes time to become accepted; purple broccoli and ruby lettuce do not sell as well as the more conventional varieties. (In fact, many people, encountering ruby lettuce in a salad in a restaurant, put it aside because they think it is spoiled). If you know your customers are unusually adventurous, you could try out new varieties and see if they are profitable; careful records of sales and costs will help you determine this.

A good and very inexpensive way to get seeds is to grow your own. While some plants—cantaloupes, for instance—may not set seeds, most do. Simply do not pick everything, but let a few plants or stems mature until they produce seeds. One vegetable spaghetti will produce a large number of seeds and one luffa sponge will have more than you and all your friends can possibly use. Certain plants—leeks and parsley, for example—will not produce seeds the first season, so you will have to wait until the following summer. This could be awkward if they are in an area scheduled to be rototilled, but most of the plants—cucumbers, squash, tomatoes—will produce seeds at the end of their growing season. These can be gathered, left to dry thoroughly, shaken out of their pods, and then carefully put in envelopes and labeled.

Keep the seeds dry and cool until the following season. The exceptions are seeds that require freezing weather to complete their cycle before germination. These can still be stored cool and dry or can be left in a cold place until they have been thoroughly frost-bitten. If you forget to do this, you can always give them a session in the freezer. Some seeds, such as parsley, that do not actually require frost will germinate much more quickly if popped in the freezer overnight before planting. Many seeds will keep several years (in fact, lotus seeds that were four hundred years old have just been found in China and have been successfully germinated), so never discard an old packet—either store-bought or home-grown—until you have tested it to see if the seeds will germinate.

To Test Seeds

It is very easy to test seeds to see if they are still alive. Simply dampen several folded-over sheets of paper toweling, put them in an aluminum pie plate or cookie sheet, and place several seeds of each variety between the sheets (labeling the groups, since you are sure to forget which is which). Wrap the pan in plastic wrap and set aside in a warm place. Look at the seeds every few days to make sure they are not molding. If they are, wash them with a little soapy water and put them in a new batch of toweling. (Wash the pans too.) If they are too small to handle easily, discard them and start with a new batch and all new materials. Depending on the length of time required to germinate (radishes and marigolds are fast, parsley is super slow), you should see some signs of a tiny shoot in anywhere from a week or two to (as with parsley) six weeks. Since many seeds take several weeks to germinate, this test could require a certain amount of patience and should be started well in advance of your planting season. Be sure to keep the toweling damp at all times and do not allow the seeds to become chilled. (If you think nothing is happening, be sure to check your germination time again before throwing out the seeds.)

You are now ready to think about planting. Your next concern is soil, and that needs a whole chapter of its own.

2. What You Need to Know About Soil

No matter where you put your garden, you will probably have soil that is not ideal. Sometimes it is too clayey, sometimes too sandy. Often—especially with urban soil—it is just so poor, both in nutrients and texture, and so compacted and full of building scrap and other debris, that it seems as if the only solution would be to dispose of it and start from scratch with good soil. Since this is rarely a practical solution, it is important to find out what kind of soil you have and how to improve it.

There is, of course, another way to go: you can garden in containers. If you have a rooftop or garden apartment, this is your only choice, and it can work out very well. Or you can approximate that in the country with container-gardening on a terrace. Another option is raised-bed gardening—which works well for city gardeners—in which you add soil for several inches above ground level; the soil mixture you add can be just what is needed.

Even if you were to start out with ideal soil, fully fertilized, you would still need to understand what soil contains and how it works, because every crop you grow depletes the soil, at least to some extent, of some essential elements. Even ideal soil, once it is used to grow crops, must be constantly replenished if optimum yield is to be maintained. Good soil management is not difficult—although it can sometimes be expensive, cash-cropping will help defray the cost—and there are only a few things you really need to know.

Texture

The first thing to determine is the texture of the soil. This can be most easily done by comparing the soil in your garden with good topsoil or at least its equivalent. Any store that has a garden center will provide you with a small bag of potting soil. When you dampen it slightly, smell it. It will have a woods-after-the-rain smell, like a well-matured compost heap. Pick up a damp handful and squeeze it gently. If it forms a ball that crumbles easily and can be trickled through your fingers, it will have the texture you are after in your garden. Soil that is too sandy will never form a ball; soil that is too clayey will never crumble and trickle through your fingers. Most good soils are fairly dark in color (although depleted soil brought up to good texture and fertility may always remain on the light side), but color alone is not a reliable guide since many depleted swamp or bog soils are almost black because of the material of which they are formed.

Now compare the potting soil with your garden soil. No matter what is wrong with the texture, clayey or sandy, the remedy is the same: add organic matter. If your soil is extremely clayey or sandy, you may not have the patience or the resources to get it into perfect shape the first season. But if you observe certain simple rules, you should be able to manage. Never walk on most soil when it is wet. It will turn to cement or its equivalent and will be hard to dig and impossible for seedlings and roots to penetrate. Very sandy soil doesn't present quite the same problem, but it will drain so quickly that it will require frequent watering in all but the rainy season. If you must site the garden in a low, wet area or where a spring runs through, you may want to deliberately make your soil sandy to prevent your plants from rotting. But in most instances sandy soil is a real bother. Along with water, nutrients are also quickly leached out and are often gone before the plant has had a chance to utilize them. This will require more frequent fertilizing—not only a chore but an expensive procedure.

To build good soil, regardless of the original problem, add all the organic matter or humus you can. Kitchen waste, including eggshells, potato and other vegetable peelings, tired lettuce and spinach leaves, orange peels and coffee grounds, is all desirable and can be dug into the garden at any time. Since you will not have enough of this unless you are running a restaurant, you can also use peat moss, well-rotted manure, and even leaves. If you want to be very professional, pile this humusy material into a compost heap, layered with manure and dampened down at regular intervals. When it starts to work, it will become hot, literally, and should be turned over every so often. If you are in too much of a hurry to create a compost heap, chop up all the material as finely as possible and simply dig it in. Avoid kitchen waste that includes fish or meat scraps; these will attract every cat and dog in the neighborhood, as well as raccoons, which will find out about the garden quickly enough without your putting up an open-house sign.

Once your soil is properly conditioned and your garden is in place, you can simplify this whole procedure by using Ruth Stout's method of mulching heavily with several inches of salt hay. All the organic material you want to incorporate can then be laid on top of the soil, under the hay, without your having to dig it in. If you do this right, you will never need to rototill, water, weed, or fertilize again after the first few years. Since my garden is just off the lane and in sight of neighbors and visitors, I have never done this. But one of these days when I get tired of spending so much time on just these four chores, I may try it and wait to see if anyone complains about the appearance of a deep mulch. For a gardener trying for cash crops, it is by far the most economical—both in time and money—of all gardening methods.

If, however, you prefer to add organic matter as you go along or as it becomes available, do not feel it must be dug in deeply each time. Rototilling will do that for you, and rain will help the nutrients from the decomposed material work down into the deeper layers of your soil.

Soil that is poor in organic matter will not attract earthworms, and earthworms are among a gardener's best friends. If you remove all your plants each fall and let the garden lie bare and barren, the earthworms will leave. If you have dug in a plentiful supply of peat moss and other organic matter, they will stay happily through the winter and go to work for you early in the spring.

Another essential to good soil is soil bacteria. Nature uses soil bacteria to break down organic matter into a form the plants can utilize. Neglected, depleted, barren soil will have few, if any, soil bacteria.

One thing to remember when putting organic matter directly into the garden (rather than on the compost heap) is that it will require a good dose of nitrogen. Decomposing matter uses nitrogen in the process and can, in the short term, deplete the soil of this absolutely essential ingredient. In the long term, everything balances out, which is fortunate, since nitrogen is the most expensive of all fertilizers. For the first year or two of this method, be sure to add nitrogen even if you need nothing else.

Gypsum added to organic matter will speed up the improvement of soil that is too clayey. Sand will work if you can't get gypsum, but gypsum is better and is not expensive. If you are container-gardening but want to use garden soil, use perlite or vermiculite instead of gypsum. They will work just as well and have the advantage of being much lighter—an important consideration if you want to move the containers around. Of the two, vermiculite is slightly more desirable because it retains water and nutrients in high proportion to its volume.

There is no rule of thumb as to quantities. You cannot add too much organic matter, so at least there is no danger of spoiling anything. If you add too little, you can tell, to some extent, by checking the texture according to the description I have given above. You will also find your yield is not as good as it should be. Do not be discouraged if it takes a couple of years to bring your soil up to maximum fertility. It took nature millions of years to create topsoil, and this is the process you are trying to hasten.

Sweet and Sour: Understanding pH

In the good old days any farmer worth his salt could tell whether a soil was sweet or sour by tasting it; it was that simple. Today the average gardener, lacking this ability, can fall back on soil tests. You can either buy a kit and do it yourself or send a sample to your local extension service office and, for a small fee, they will do it for you.

No matter which way you do it, what you will be doing is measuring the pH, or acid/alkaline condition, of the soil. This measure is expressed in terms of numbers from 1 to 14. A pH of 7 is neutral; below 7 the soil is acid; above 7 it is alkaline. Neither extreme is desirable. Some plants and vegetables require a slightly more acid or alkaline soil than others, but unless you are a perfectionist and want to drive yourself crazy, you can grow most vegetables around the neutral mark. Certain plants, such as laurels or rhododendrons, require soil that is too acid for most vegetables, and that is why I do not recommend combining vegetables and acid-loving plants in the same bed. Lilacs, on the other hand, like an alkaline soil and will combine with certain crops.

If tests determine that your soil is too sweet (alkaline) or too sour (acid), it is not difficult to change it. Along with its analysis the extension service will include a specific recommendation as to what and how much to add. If you are using a kit, it is fairly simple to change the pH. If your soil is too acid, add lime; it is cheap and widely available. Be sure it is dolomite lime, which will not burn and which contains magnesium and calcium, which are valuable trace elements.

If your soil is too alkaline, add more organic matter. The Department of Agriculture also recommends aluminum sulfate. This will work more quickly than organic matter, but it is not recommended for the organic gardener. Organic matter is not only free, it will add many other valuable nutrients to the soil. Besides, if you condition your soil in the fall and let it lie fallow over the winter, it will be ready in the spring even with organic matter.

Many gardeners lime and fertilize at the same time. This is not a good idea, because the lime will cancel out the benefit of some of the fertilizer and you will have no way of knowing whether or not you have added enough. Leave a month, if possible, between both treatments, and apply the lime first.

Organic vs Inorganic Fertilizers

This decision must be made when you decide what kind of fertilizer to use. It must be made again when you are confronted with garden pests—but the first encounter is with fertilizers.

Regardless of whether your fertilizers are organic or inorganic, they will be chosen for certain specific nutrients. The three that are most important and needed in the largest quantity are nitrogen, phosphorus, and potassium. The simplest and most efficient way to buy them is in that combination, and bags of this trio are available in all garden centers. The proportions are not, however, always the same; the bag will carry information about the contents clearly marked in the form of numbers. For instance, "5–10–10" on a bag tells you that the bag contains 5 percent nitrogen, 10 percent phosphorus, and 10 percent potassium. If you are buying a 50-pound bag, you will get $2\frac{1}{2}$ pounds of nitrogen, 5 pounds of phosphorus, and 5 pounds of potassium. This obviously does not add up to 100 percent, because most of the contents of the bag is filler. Since the elements in the fertilizers are always listed alphabetically, you will recognize that a 10–5–10 formula means 10 percent nitrogen, 5 percent phosphorus, and 5 percent potassium. You can usually save money by buying the lower nitrogen mixture and mixing nitrogen into the fertilizer you use for leafy crops. The 5–10–10 formula is best for root crops. The most commonly used formula is 5–10–5; additional fertilizers can be used to beef this up where needed.

Here are some sources of individual fertilizers.

Fertilizer	What It Does	Organic	Inorganic
Nitrogen	Promotes leafy top growth	cottonseed meal dried blood	ureaform nitrate of soda calcium nitrate
Phosphorus	Strong stem and feeder roots; fruit set	bonemeal rock phosphate	superphosphate
Potassium	Healthy storage roots; makes plants winter-hardy	wood ash greensand granite dust	potassium chloride muriate of potash

A soil analysis will best determine whether your soil has a particular deficiency. In using fertilizer, it is better to fertilize little and often than to overfertilize at any time. While, generally speaking, organic fertilizers will not burn plants or cause them to spurt into growth in an unnatural way, it is still better to keep nutrients coming at an even rate. Special conditions, such as an exceptionally rainy spell, may require a stepped-up fertilizer schedule. Just ordinary common sense will tell you when to follow the rules and when to make an exception.

There is no question in my mind that organic fertilizers are more desirable. You need only consider that a soil treated solely with inorganic fertilizers loses its soil bacteria, which have nothing to work with, and its own natural fertility. The soil becomes merely a holding mechanism for the fertilizer you apply, and there is no carry-over benefit or improvement of the soil itself. You become locked into an increasingly expensive and vicious circle and must add inorganic fertilizers from then on if you wish to grow anything at all. Fortunately, you can switch to organic fertilizers at any time.

Organic fertilizers, whether they are from your kitchen, your compost heap, or your garden store, improve the soil at the same time that they bring nutrients to your plants. They encourage the growth of earthworms and soil bacteria, decrease the gardener's work, and are pleasant to use. They also take care of a great deal of "garbage" at a time when we are running out of places to dump it.

In addition, there is an important but hidden advantage to organic fertilizers: they contain trace elements. As our biological technology is becoming more sophisticated, we are finding out that we have underestimated the importance of trace elements to human health. Only recently did we discover that zinc was a vitally important trace element and that the majority of Americans have a zinc deficiency. If you use inorganic fertilizers, made in a factory from petroleum products, you may get the chemical equivalent of the element you are buying—whether nitrogen, phosphorus, or potassium—but you will not get the hidden trace elements that are in organic matter. You will not get them partly because it would be costly to add them and partly because we do not even know, in many cases, that they exist. Of those with which we are now familiar, we have often not yet been able to determine in what quantity they are required. Nature knows and will supply us with what we need if we give her half a chance. Growing vegetables organically means getting the nutrients you need without having to figure out what they are.

At this point you may say that tests have shown that vegetables grown in inorganic fertilizer or even in depleted soil still manage to provide us with all the nutrients to be found in organically grown vegetables. Well, yes and no. In researching one of my garden books, *Grow Your Own Chinese Vegetables,* (Macmillan, 1978), I came on a Department of Agriculture memorandum describing tests that had proved organically grown vegetables actually did contain more nutrients and poor soil produced less nutritive crops. Unfortunately I cannot at this moment put my hands on it again (my files need some work), and the Department of Agriculture tends to go somewhat blank when I refer to it, but it does exist. Even if it didn't, I'm afraid I would still feel that it must be so and that good soil produces good, more nutritive vegetables and that chemicals at any stage of growth are not good for living things. A few years ago *The New York Times* ran a lengthy article saying that vegetables grown with organic fertilizers have now definitely been shown to be higher in vitamins and minerals. Since then many other articles have appeared to say that this is at least probable. You certainly have nothing to lose and everything to gain if you go with organic gardening.

From a marketing standpoint, consumers have become so health- and nutrition-conscious that you can turn organic gardening into cash and can ask higher prices for produce you identify as organically grown—not to mention the fact that you will then be able to sell to health-food stores at their prices.

Gardening organically in terms of fertilizers is comparatively easy; it is harder when you try to deal with pests the same way. If, however, you consider that gardeners in the old days used comparatively few pest controls (and most of those were organic) and had nowhere near the pest problems we have today, you have to wonder whether we have not outsmarted ourselves. Pesticides are expensive, unpleasant to use, and questionable on edible material.

Try some of the simpler organic methods, such as red-pepper solutions and salt water (especially effective on cabbage worms), before you resort to harsher methods. Fortunately most of the cash crops I talk about in this book are fairly free of pests or can be bought in varieties that are pest-resistant.

Choosing Crops
That Count

3. Vegetables and Fruits for Cash Crops

In selecting the crops in the next two chapters, I have chosen those that are either familiar to the consumer but expensive in the market or unfamiliar and somewhat exotic but having desirable characteristics that should make them eminently marketable. In addition, most of them are easy to grow, comparatively pest-free, and prolific. If you are considering a crop with which you are not familiar, read through the description of its appearance and cultural requirements to see whether it might fit in with your gardening plans. In many instances, additional suggestions for marketing a crop can be found in the marketing section.

Asparagus Pea (*Psophocarpus tetragonolobus*)

If you have never grown asparagus peas, you are in for a pleasant surprise. They are so easy to grow that they even beat out the weeds and will be happy in almost any soil—and just about every part of the plant is edible. In fact, it has been called "supermarket on a stalk" because it combines the characteristics of so many vegetables. The leaves can be eaten like spinach and contain the same nutritive value; the flowers when sautéed taste like mushrooms; the immature pods taste like asparagus-flavored green beans; the immature seeds can be eaten like peas; the mature dry seeds can be roasted and eaten or processed like soybeans, and are even more nutritious than soybeans. And if all that isn't enough, the roots are similar to sweet potatoes but higher in protein.

Once you have discovered this extraordinary legume you will wonder why it isn't a staple in every garden. Actually, although it has been known for centuries in the East, it has only recently been brought to this hemisphere. Of the over eight hundred known types, only a few will grow in the temperate climate, because most types will not flower during long days; also, the vegetable was looked down on as rather plebeian just because it was so prolific and easy to grow. At the present time the only seed catalogs in which I have found it are Thompson & Morgan and Park (see Appendix B for addresses), but keep an eye out for it—it will probably start appearing in many more catalogs.

The asparagus pea is easy to prepare for eating; depending upon which part you have chosen, you can boil, stir-fry, steam, bake, or eat it raw. The flowers, for instance, can be sautéed briefly or added to a salad for a colorful and tasty nibble. Even the roots can be eaten, raw as well as boiled, baked, roasted, or fried.

Since the plant is so easy to grow and so prolific, you can market it in any number of ways. Introducing an unfamiliar vegetable is a little different from simply selling a crop for which there is already a market. The disadvantage is that you will have to do a bit of an educating job—possibly even to persuade the produce manager to carry it. One easy way to convince him is to prepare a dish with the vegetable and bring it to him to taste, along with your crop already packaged. If you are as good a cook as you are a gardener, the asparagus pea will sell itself. (Health-food stores and specialty food shops are usually receptive to new foods and recipes.) Your next step is to prepare some literature —it can simply be a typed or legibly handwritten sheet—that tells a little about the nutritional, high-protein qualities of this extraordinary vegetable and offers some very, very simple suggestions for its use. If you are growing it for the first time yourself, experiment with packaging it; some parts, such as the flowers, may not stand up for long enough to be stocked in the market. In that case you may either keep them for your own enjoyment or sell them directly to the consumer, picking them when you have an order.

Appearance

The asparagus pea grows, like English peas and snow peas, on a twining vine. It can reach as high as 13 feet, in which case it will have to have something to grow on, just as other peas do. It is possible, however, to grow the Thompson & Morgan variety, which never becomes taller than 12 inches. This variety does not require staking and has handsome reddish-russet flowers rather than the usual blue ones. It forms a very decorative plot in the garden and does not grow as rampant as the vines. If, however, you get a variety that grows tall, remember you can interplant it with corn, and the vines will use the dead cornstalks just as pole beans do.

Another name for the asparagus pea—although I have never seen it used in this country—is winged bean. This name derives from the exotic appearance of the pods, which are unlike any other I know of. The pods are four-sided, somewhat square, with winged projections. The shape is so clearly defined that it is apparent even when the pods are sliced vertically (as for stir-frying or steaming), which makes it a real conversation piece for a company meal—something one does not expect of a mere vegetable. Add to this the delectable taste and you will find it is a popular dish for special occasions (although you eat it daily because the plant is so prolific).

When to Plant

The asparagus pea is not particularly sensitive to frost and can be planted as early as two weeks before the last frost in your area. If you are tempted to plant earlier—as I often am—you have nothing to lose except a few minutes of your time and a packet of seeds. Most of the time I find the gamble works, and then I am rewarded with an earlier crop.

Where to Plant

Since the leaves are succulent, they would undoubtedly appeal to rabbits and other animal pests (anything that eats my plants is a pest), but I have always grown them in a fenced-in area, so I am not speaking from experience. I would strongly suggest you put them in your regular vegetable garden.

How to Plant

The seeds are easy to plant because they are large enough to handle individually. They should be set half an inch deep, about 6 inches apart, in rows 18 inches apart. In practice I cheat a little and put the rows much closer. If you do this, you will find they form a green intertwined mat, and you have to hunt a little harder to harvest the immature pods (if that is what you want). I still prefer this method because it increases the yield considerably.

If you have prepared the soil with some compost, well-rotted manure, and 10–10–10 fertilizer dug in before planting, you do not really have to fertilize again. The asparagus pea has host bacteria that grow on its roots and that fix atmospheric nitrogen in a form that the plant can convert to food. Because of this characteristic, any part of the plant that remains after harvest, such as the stalk, should be dug into the garden soil and allowed to return its nitrogen as it decomposes.

The nitrogen-fixing ability of the asparagus pea also makes it tolerant of poor soil conditions. Thompson & Morgan calls it "the grow-anywhere pea," which gives you some example of how undemanding it is. It is one of the few vegetables that will grow in both sandy and clayey soils. If you want a really good crop, however, I suspect a little attention to basic soil conditions will pay off.

Culture

Once firmly established, the asparagus pea will take over its area, and weeds will have a hard time competing. To quote Thompson & Morgan again, "It will beat the weeds if you sow it and forget it."

The only care that will be required on your part is a little watering during dry weather. In its original habitat most of the varieties were moisture-loving, and I find that a little extra water during dry spells is appreciated.

Harvest

The leaves and flowers can, of course, be harvested as soon as they appear, but discretion is advised if you are not to eat up the plant before it has had time to reach its full potential. If you have resisted and have allowed the pods to form, they should be harvested when immature and about one inch long. If they are any longer, you will have to string them like green beans and they will not have the delicate asparaguslike flavor from which they take their name. The pods will be ready to pick about 50 days after sowing.

If you want to eat the "peas," they should be left to form to the bumpy stage, but do not let them mature—unless that is the way you want to eat them.

Strangely enough, the roots may be ready earlier than the pods; you might dig down to check as early as 35 to 50 days after sowing. They are best when not left to the end of the season.

If you pick the vegetable in the immature pod stage, you will find you can crop steadily for about ten weeks. This is especially good when you are introducing a new vegetable because it gives people time to try it and come back for more. I would suggest that you experiment, eating various parts of the plant prepared in various ways, so that you can decide for yourself which will be the most popular part and use. I would suggest also that you do not attempt to promote all the many aspects of the plant but gradually introduce them over several seasons.

Once you have a good crop, be sure to let some mature so that you have seeds for next year. Because it is a novelty still, the seed packets are not inexpensive, especially considering the small number of seeds in a packet, and you will do much better saving your seed from one season to the next.

Belgian Endive (*Cichorium intybus*)

Growing Belgian endive is a little more complicated than growing most of the other plants we discuss in this book. It is, however, well worth it, both because it is a delicious and versatile vegetable and because it can provide a cash crop during the winter months. It also is a crop that commands a luxury price in any market and can offer you a good rate of return. Once you have set up a system for the necessary indoor growing period, there is nothing to prevent you from providing the local markets with a constant supply. Like so many high-priced vegetables, Belgian endive is remarkably easy to grow, and the fact that you do not have to count a high air fare from Belgium into your selling costs means your margin of profit is exceptionally large. If you wish, you could even undercut the current market price and still do very well indeed.

Appearance

Belgian endive appears in the market as tightly headed, cigar-shaped cones of delicately pale, cream-colored leaves. In fact, one of its other names, witloof chicory, means "white-leaved chicory."

When looking in seed catalogs to order it, do not confuse this vegetable with the salad greens commonly called endive. Under the heading of "endive" you will find descriptions for various kinds of escarole, with its broad green-and-white leaves, and green curled endive, which has deeply cut and curly green leaves. You will have to look under "witloof chicory," although you may occasionally find it listed under "chicon" (the name of the second-stage cones) or "Belgian endive," "Flemish endive," or "French endive." The term you will encounter most often is "witloof chicory."

A horizontal method of culturing the mature roots will grow a crop of what is known as *barbes-de-capucin*, which are loose rather than headed shoots. You will find this described in French seed catalogs, but I do not think the market for this vegetable is as good for a cash crop as the standard Belgian endive, because it is totally unfamiliar to most Americans.

In its first stage of growth, in your outdoor garden, you may be surprised to find that witloof chicory looks exactly like the weedy plant with the pretty blue flower that grows along the roadside and in abandoned fields. It is the same plant. This should tell you how easy it is to grow, since it springs up in poor soil and spreads uncared for under the worst possible conditions. It may interest you to know also that the roots are the same variety of chicory that is used to add flavor to coffee, a mixture that is particularly popular in France. If you wish to use chicory roots as a coffee substitute, I suggest you harvest the wild roots; save your garden plants for your endive crop.

When to Plant

Belgian endive seeds should be sown directly in the ground in early summer when the ground has warmed up. This begins the first stage.

Where to Plant

This is a crop for your vegetable garden, but the mature plant will be about 18 inches tall, so be sure to put it where it will not shade plants that require full sun. It can be placed so as to shade lettuce, cress, and other plants that can use some protection from midsummer heat.

How to Plant

Since this is actually a root crop, prepare the soil deeply, digging in compost, well-rotted manure, and fertilizer that is high in phosphorus and potash. The roots grow fairly long (like winter radishes or parsnips), so deep digging will reward you with strong, healthy roots.

Sow the seed thinly and cover lightly with fine soil or sand in rows about 18 inches apart. When the seedlings are a few inches high, thin to stand about 12 inches apart. You can transplant the extra seedlings, if you wish, when they are about 3 inches high; if you wait until they get taller, the roots will be too deep to work with. If you do not wish to transplant them, you can use them as an especially delicate salad green.

Culture

In the first stage the culture of Belgian endive is as easy as growing weeds. Even weeding is required only when the seedlings are first getting started; once they have taken hold they will discourage the growth of any weeds in their immediate vicinity. Water freely in dry periods and fertilize lightly when the plants are about six weeks old; most of the fertilizer required by the roots should already be in place before you sow.

The second stage of growing Belgian endive is the interesting one. Since it is not frost-hardy, this must take place either in the house proper or in a cellar that is not too cool.

In the fall, when the plant matures, or earlier if it seems about to go to seed (you may want to let a few plants go to seed so that you will not have to buy any the following June), dig up the roots. Do this carefully; they will be deep, and you should not break or bruise them. A good idea is to dig with a fork spade along the row and then come in around each plant until the ground has been thoroughly loosened. At that point you may be able to pull up the root by hand by tugging gently on the top of the plant that is above the ground.

Once all the roots are dug, trim off the tops, leaving an inch to an inch and a half above the crown. Then trim off the slender tips, if any, and cut the roots to a uniform length, usually 8 or 9 inches. Remove any side shoots and divide the roots into those you wish to force right away for a crop and the ones you want to store for later use.

The roots you are holding over for a later crop should go into cold storage—that is, cold enough to prevent sprouting but not so cold as to freeze. To keep them from drying out during the storage period, put them in containers of dry sand; they can be layered horizontally so one box will hold a good number.

The roots you wish to use to grow Belgian endive are now ready to be planted. You will need a container that is approximately twice as deep as the roots. The depth is needed so you can plant the roots and still have room for the top growth. I use medium-sized plastic garbage cans, which look neat, are easy to clean, and are just about the right size for a good crop. You can use as many of these as you need for the crop you wish to produce; since the yield is predictable—one endive per root—it is easy to plan how many to force at a time.

The roots should be placed upright, with the crown on top, touching one another, as closely packed as possible. Then all spaces should be filled in with damp sand. It is important that the sand be as damp as possible but not wet; if it is wet, the roots may rot. Put in enough damp sand to cover the roots.

The next step is to provide a protective blanching medium for the growing shoots. To do this you will need to add about 6 to 8 inches of dry sand. The sand must be perfectly dry; its only function is to blanch the shoots. Do not cover this sand but leave it open to the air.

Recently I have noticed that Thompson & Morgan feature a Belgian endive they list as "chicon," which can be propagated in the second stage in a large flowerpot without a second layer of sand but with merely the protection of a second flowerpot inverted over the first to exclude the light. The method is illustrated in their catalog and would probably prove satisfactory for a small crop. If your indoor space for this sort of thing is limited, it might be worth looking into.

Harvest

In about a month after setting in the roots you will see little, delicate shoots here and there above the dry sand. With a sharp paring knife gently work your way down to the bottom of the shoot—about six inches. Cut it off just above the crown of the root, being reasonably careful not to cut into the crown, and you will have a Belgian endive. You will find the entire crop matures at about the same time. Once you have cut out all the mature endives, you have a choice. If you are selling the crop, you may wish to discard the roots and plant new ones from your cold-storage containers. If you have been good about selling all of this first crop, you may want to reward yourself with some for your own table. To do this, make sure the bottom level of sand is still damp. If it is not, water it lightly, and then leave the top dry sand in place. A second crop of shoots will reward your patience. The heads won't be perfectly compact—in fact, some of them may be quite loose, so they won't be as marketable—but they will have the same delicious flavor and you will benefit from getting twice the yield: a cash crop and one for your own table.

Incidentally, if you find the demand is not as great as the amount you can grow, you can increase the demand by acquainting people with the delights of braised Belgian endive. Simply include a recipe for this in the area where the endive is sold. You will find that braised endive is addictive and that a person who has tried it once will not be able to resist making it again. Since people tend to eat much larger portions of braised endive than endive used in salad, you will increase your sales considerably.

Garlic (*Allium sativum*)

Garlic is so useful, both as a medicine and as a food, that it should be in everyone's garden so that it can be used freely without regard to cost. It is a staple in the produce market, and you will get an especially good price if you sell it to health-food stores that sell fresh vegetables. (Of course, in order to do this you must be sure to grow it organically—but you ought to anyway.)

Man has known about garlic since the beginning of time; in fact, it is so ancient that botanists cannot determine when or where it originated. It is no surprise that such an ancient vegetable has developed its own mythology, but modern scientists have found that many of the folkloric uses for garlic stand up under scientific investigation. Some of its properties, however, have been more difficult to substantiate. Even modern scientific investigation has been unable to determine whether it will truly protect fair damsels from vampires or whether witches will really vanish at the sight of it. Perhaps, however, none of the folk tales are as amazing as the recent discovery that a drop of garlic juice in a gallon of water is an effective mosquito spray—more effective, in fact, than many of the insecticides that have unpleasant side effects on the user.

In modern times garlic has been credited with reducing high blood pressure, preventing infections, and reducing the incidence of the flu and colds. It appears to speed up the healing of wounds when used in a poultice applied directly to the site and was extensively used by Russian soldiers during World War II for this purpose. Since it also prevents infections when used this way, it eliminates the need for costly over-the-counter preparations.

In addition, it is an essential ingredient in the foods of almost every country in the world. It is hard to imagine how a good cook would manage without its delicious flavor; whether it is used cold or hot, in salads or stir-fry dishes.

To present it for selling is no problem since it is usually sold loose in baskets or bins from which the customer makes a selection of bulbs. If, however, you want to do something a little special, you could braid the tops together and create strings of various lengths, or you could work the tops into braided ribbons with a loop and a bow on top for hanging. Another traditional way of displaying garlic is to take a spray of wheat stalks, or even hay, and, with string, tie the garlic bulbs to it in four rows.

If you plan to use any of these suggestions, decide before you store the garlic, since you would otherwise remove both the roots and the tops. Ropes of garlic will command a higher price than the same number of bulbs sold in bulk. You will have to invest more of your own labor in making them and you also will have to figure in the cost of any materials (ribbons, for example), but the price you can charge will be well worth your efforts and added expense. The local market had some garlic braids for sale today, and I counted 21 bulbs in the string that sold for over $8.00.

Appearance

Garlic grows in the form of bulbs that are made up of a number—usually 10 or 12—of individual cloves. Recipes usually describe how much garlic is needed (when it is more than a minced teaspoon or two) in terms of the number of cloves.

Each clove and the outside of the bulb are encased in a thin papery skin that protects the delicate flesh. The skin is usually removed before cooking, although some people claim you can toss the whole clove into a pot without removing the skin. I have never quite had the courage to risk this, so I cannot report whether or not it is satisfactory. It is, however, very easy to remove the skin if you simply flatten the clove with the flat side of a knife blade. The clove will get slightly mashed and the skin will drop off in your fingers.

Garlic comes both white and pink or purplish. If you are ordering the bulbs from a seed company, you may not have a choice. But if you are buying your planting bulbs from the market, pick out the pink or purplish ones; they tend to keep longer than the white. Always be careful to gently press on the bulbs when selecting them; there are always some that have dried out and will feel light and not solid. These are useless and will have to be discarded. Do not buy a bulb that has any cloves in this condition or you may find that none of them will sprout.

If you want to try marketing a new product on a small scale (you could start with just one adventurous market), plant a couple of flowerpots with garlic cloves. When the green shoots are about three inches high, start snipping them in small quantities—just as you would chives—and freeze them. You will soon have enough to put in small packages and label "garlic-flavored chives." These add a pleasant, delicate garlic flavor to salads, garlic bread, and cooked dishes and are great to sprinkle on fish and egg dishes. If you look in the freezer section of your market you will see ordinary chives packaged this way. The price will amaze you, and you will get an idea of how to package your garlic chives. The market probably won't object to giving you the freezer space, because the packages are small, the price is right, and you will be offering the cachet of introducing a new gourmet product.

When to Plant

Garlic may be planted in either early spring or late fall (for spring harvesting).

Where to Plant

Garlic can be planted anywhere it is convenient—in the vegetable or herb garden or in the flower beds. I plant it with my roses to keep away aphids and other pests and put rows of it around any small flower or vegetable beds that are not fenced, because none of the animals like it and they seem to keep out of plantings that are ringed with it. Maybe they nibble on it and the taste discourages them from any taste tests deeper into the bed. I have not tried it as protection against anything as tempting as lettuce, but I have not had any problem in any of the beds in which I have used it. Lately, since baby woodchucks have been getting into my fenced vegetable garden, I plant it—along with bunching onions and Chinese chives—

around the inside of the fence, and so far (crossed fingers) it has worked.

The foliage is attractive enough to put anywhere, so your choice is wide.

You will want to be sure that the site receives full sun and the soil is suitable for a root vegetable—light and friable and not clayey.

How to Plant

Divide the bulbs into cloves and plant right side up, with the pointed tip at the top about 1 to $1\frac{1}{2}$ inches deep. The cloves should be set about 4 inches apart in rows 12 inches apart. Firm the soil over the cloves and keep well watered during dry spells. If you have had trouble growing radishes or other root vegetables in that area, add fertilizer rich in phosphorus and potash rather than the usual 5–10–5.

Culture

Keep the area around the bulbs weeded and water as needed. Fertilize with a bead of fertilizer dropped along the row twice during the growing season. You won't have much of a problem with pests— either insect or animal—so this is a carefree crop for the busy gardener.

Harvest

Garlic takes about four months to mature. It usually tells you when it is ready to be harvested, because the tops turn tan and fall over. If, however, your soil is very rich, or for any number of other reasons (not all of which we know), the tops may not fall over when they should. In this case, check the size of the bulbs by digging carefully down alongside of them and brushing away the soil to check on the growth. If the bulb seems large enough, bend the tops over with a rake and leave them until they have turned tan and are drying out.

Then dig the bulbs up carefully and leave on top of the ground to dry in the sun for a day or so. If it looks like rain, move them to an airy spot under cover. Once they are thoroughly dry, cut off the tops and trim the roots if necessary. Remember not to do this to those you want to save for braiding.

Store in a cool dry place, just like onions.

Special Note

There is a special variety of garlic that grows to an enormous size—you won't believe it until you see it. It is called variously Jumbo Garlic and Elephant Garlic. You won't find it in the stores—which is a good reason for you to grow it and sell it—and not all seed catalogs list it. Nichols and Thompson & Morgan are two that do, but check your favorite catalog, which may also have it. You may find this variety shipped only in the fall for spring harvesting, so look it up before you work it into your garden plan.

The flavor is much milder than that of ordinary garlic—for the same reason, I guess, that large onions are milder and sweeter than small onions—and it should appeal to cooks who like a little garlic flavor but usually find it overpowering.

If you grow and sell this interesting vegetable, you might want to prepare a little tag or slip telling of its special qualities and introducing it to the consumer. Needless to say, it should be premium-priced—although, of course, it is no harder to grow than any other variety of garlic.

Horseradish (*Armoracia lapathifolia*)

I do not know whether animals in the wild season their meals with bites of spicy leaves and berries to make their food more interesting, but humans certainly do. And high among my favorite ways of adding interest to food is freshly grated horseradish.

Long before botanists kept track of such things, horseradish was known and used throughout Eastern Europe. It was thought to be healthful as well as tasty and was used as a specific treatment for rheumatism. In modern times it has come down as one of the "bitter herbs" associated with the Passover ritual meal.

Down through the ages horseradish escaped or was carried by colonists—as in the case of the British, who brought it to America—until today it is found growing wild throughout most of the world. It has also found its way into many different cuisines, and in this country is popularly used for such diverse dishes as shrimp cocktail, for which it makes a pungent sauce, and New England boiled dinner, which otherwise would be very bland. While horseradish has a particular affinity for boiled beef and shellfish, it is also enjoyed by the Irish with their corned beef and lends its virtues to numerous other dishes.

Horseradish is most commonly served grated into white vinegar or lemon juice, alone or mixed with grated turnip or beets. Most Americans do not know that, cooked like parsnips, it makes an excellent braised vegetable. If your only experience of horseradish has been the processed, bottled variety available in most markets, your first taste of your own freshly grated variety, with a touch of vinegar, will be a revelation. It was once possible, before your time and mine, to get freshly grated horseradish on the streets of New York City. Special vendors, equipped with horseradish roots and grating machines, stood on street corners and grated a bottleful to order. I understand that this was the only acceptable way for those knowledgeable about the joys of horseradish to buy it. Now that I have eaten my own, I understand why these old-timers look with such disdain on the products available at the local supermarket.

The problem with the bottled variety, aside from the possibility that it may have unnecessary additives, is that there is no way of determining its freshness. Sometimes color can be a guide; fresh horseradish is snow-white, and only gradually does it acquire the gray tinge that warns the buyer it will not do. As it discolors, it also loses strength, flavor, and freshness. If you store a bottle in the refrigerator for any length of time, you can watch for yourself how the color changes.

Obviously, a product that has a limited shelf life is a natural money crop for the home gardener. With a small horseradish plot you can easily supply the local markets with a steady supply of freshly grated horseradish. In no time at all, as customers try your superior product, you will sell all you can process, and the national brands will gather dust, unsold, in the dairy department.

Packaging your horseradish will require bottles; the grated horseradish must be mixed with vinegar or lemon juice. Since these bottles are not returnable, the cost of the bottles should be figured into your selling price as an ongoing expense. A bit of shopping around on your part will soon find a bottle supplier who will work with your small orders in the beginning. As your sales increase, larger bulk orders will get you a lower bottle price and this can be realized as pure profit; there is no need to lower a retail price for an item that is already selling well at that level.

As customers become familiar with your plain horseradish, you can, if you wish, expand into a whole line of flavored horseradishes—but by then you will be a successful entrepreneur and will no longer need my suggestions. Do, however, pay attention to your labeling. Since you will be competing with an already established product—commercially bottled horseradish—your product will sell faster if you take the time to tell the consumer why it is better. The first taste will tell him or her; the problem is selling the first bottle. A quick way of making your point might be to date your bottles. This means you must take it upon yourself to remove any "old" bottles, but the little extra trouble is an inexpensive bit of promotion on your part, and eventually, as you learn how many bottles will sell during the various seasons, you may prefer to deliver a slightly smaller order so that your horseradish sells out every week. You need not worry that you will lose sales to customers who will buy another brand if yours is not available. The difference in taste between homegrown, freshly grated horseradish and the ordinary store-bought variety is so great that your customers will soon prefer to wait for your brand rather than buy what they will look upon as an inferior relish.

The unique "hotness" of horseradish has led to its being given various names in other countries. In England, for instance, it is often called red cole. This name derives presumably from its being a relative of the cole vegetable family. I prefer to think of it as a descriptive, Early English spelling of "red coal"—a tribute to its taste.

Appearance

There is nothing particularly attractive about the horseradish plant. Its leaves are broad, flat, and rather coarse-looking; they grow about two feet high and are said to be poisonous. The root itself is usually a straight, rather ordinary-looking taproot, not unlike a parsnip root but without that certain delicacy that distinguishes the latter. All in all, I can only think that the endearing properties of horseradish must have been discovered by some absent-minded Stone Age man nibbling on a root while thinking of something else. There is no clue in its appearance to its being of any culinary interest.

When to Plant

Horseradish is a perennial, so you need plant it only one season to enjoy it practically forever. Since it is completely winter-hardy, it can be planted in early spring as soon as the ground can be worked. Once you have an established bed as a source of new root cuttings, you can dig and plant the new cuttings as late in the fall as you please.

Where to Plant

Since horseradish is not decorative, it has no place in the flower bed. It is also not a good choice for a vegetable garden that has an annual rototilling schedule. In fact, since it is also a very invasive plant and will take over an area fairly soon, it is best given either its own private corner or controlled with a barrier of metal stripping dug into the ground and peeking up just at ground level.

Horseradish is not truly fussy, but it does like a moist soil and will do especially well on the bank of a brook or creek. Since, however, I do not have such a site, I water as often as I can and have found the crop still manages very well.

How to Plant

Like all root vegetables, horseradish likes a deep, well-prepared soil, free of tree roots, rocks, small pebbles, and other possible obstructions. Digging deeply and incorporating compost, well-rotted manure and fertilizer is well worth while, since the bed may lie undisturbed for several seasons.

Once the ground has been prepared, the planting holes can be most easily created with a round pole or crowbar. Poke your tool down deeply at a slant into the ground. Drop the root cutting into it and fill with soil. Since the root cuttings should be about 6 inches long and the top of the cutting about 4 inches from the soil surface, you can see that you need a fairly deep hole.

A word about the root cuttings. In the beginning you may get these from your seedsman, but after your first planting your bed should provide all the stock needed. In taking root cuttings from an established bed, look for lateral roots growing near the surface. When these lateral roots are as thick as a pencil, or thicker, they can be cut from the main root without damaging it. In addition, the main root often divides, and the divisions can be cut and planted. Cuttings are usually trimmed to six-inch lengths, with flat tops on the thick end and a slanted tip on the thin end. They should be planted with the slanted tip pointing down and should be set in the hole at a slight slant.

Culture

One of the easiest crops to produce, horseradish will take care of itself entirely if it has to. If, however, you want maximum production, keep the soil on the moist side and fertilize with both deep and side-dressing types of application. When using a hole-poker in deep fertilizing, it is important to try to damage as few lateral roots as possible.

It is important also to keep the bed as weed-free as possible; an easy way to do this is with deep mulch around the plants. Almost anything that shelters the ground from the sun will do; hay, compost, grass, black plastic, even newspapers laid thickly and covered with a bit of grass or hay for appearance's sake.

Harvest

Roots planted in the spring will yield harvest by fall, but since the best growth is made in cool fall weather, the longer you can leave a first planting, the better both the quality and quantity of your crop will be. Since the plant is not tender, a deep mulch directly over it will allow you to dig roots all winter—a useful feature for the gardener who wants to sell produce year round.

If you are not overfond of digging through the snow to reach the ground and the roots, it is possible to store roots in your freezer indefinitely. When ready to grate, simply take out a frozen root, grate without thawing, and return whatever is left of the root to the freezer for the next time. The grated root will thaw enough to squeeze out in no time and can then be mixed with vinegar or lemon juice, just like the fresh root.

Hot Peppers (*Capsicum frutescens*)

Hot pepper plants are so beautiful that they are used as ornamental house plants; the variety sold by florists, with their glossy dark-green leaves, blossoms and fruit on the same plant at the same time, and the various colors of the ripening peppers, are just as edible as the ones grown in the vegetable garden. In fact, if you happen to have an ornamental pepper plant in your living room, the day you run out of hot peppers and want to make chili, you can use the peppers from that plant. All hot peppers are edible and all are ornamental in appearance.

Hot peppers are native to America and were discovered by Columbus. He promptly brought them back to Europe, where they were useful in hiding the slightly off taste so often found in meat in those days of no refrigeration. Soon thereafter Portuguese sailors introduced them to the Far East. Hot peppers were so completely incorporated into Oriental cooking that in later years botanists thought they were native to the East.

In recent years their popularity has increased rather than diminished, and they are now widely used in South American, Mexican, and American cooking as well as in Oriental cooking, such as Hunan and Szechwan. They are also considered very healthful, and the lower incidence of certain diseases in Texas is ascribed partly to their wide use in Texan cooking.

Hot peppers are especially suited to the home gardener who would like a little cash crop on the side, because they take up comparatively little space, can be put in the flower garden if room is needed in the vegetable garden for less ornamental but essential vegetables, and are so prolific that even a few plants will produce a large number of peppers.

Appearance

Pepper plants form small, compact bushes of dark green, glossy leaves. Once they start to bear, they will fruit and flower at the same time, so that you will have green, yellow, and bright red fruit, hanging down like Christmas tree ornaments, while the white flowers are sprinkled throughout the foliage. They are neat and interesting in the vegetable garden, pretty in the flower bed, and make handsome house plants.

There are many varieties of hot peppers. Most turn red when mature, but some go through a very attractive yellow stage. One variety I have grown with great pleasure is a miniature bush with very lovely tiny peppers that turn purple on maturity. Since they take up so little room, you can afford to experiment.

For sale, they can be packaged in trays, strung on strings to sell as dried peppers, or incorporated into wreaths or dried flower arrangements. In addition, if you talk to your local florist, you may find you can pot them after your outdoor growing season and sell them as house plants. If you are even more ambitious, you can make and bottle your own hot pepper oil.

When to Plant

Hot peppers are sensitive to cold, so they can be started indoors and then set out in the garden when all danger of frost has passed and the soil has warmed up. They are very easy to transplant. Often, however, if I am too busy to start seed indoors, I take a chance and plant the seeds in the open garden. I usually put black plastic over the seedbed until the seeds germinate and then use a shell of clear plastic to cover the seedlings if the nights are cool. If you put the black plastic down a week before you put in your seeds, the soil will be much warmer than if you left it uncovered. I also water in the beginning with warm tap water, but this is not practical unless you have only a small planting. If you want to plant directly in the ground, choose earlier varieties as well as the regular ones so you won't have so long to wait.

Where to Plant

As I have mentioned, hot peppers can be planted just about anywhere. Of course, like all vegetables, they require full sun but otherwise are not too demanding. Hot peppers do have one peculiarity of which the vegetable gardener must be aware: they should not be planted next to sweet peppers or they may turn the sweet peppers hot. This is due to cross-pollination, since the "hot" element is transmitted through the seeds—as anyone knows who has accidentally eaten some chili pepper seeds. I frequently plant hot and sweet peppers in contiguous beds and have never had this happen, but it is a possibility.

How to Plant

Pepper seeds are easy to handle, so you can easily seed 12 to a flat for transplanting. The seedlings should be set 18 to 20 inches apart in rows 20 to 16 inches apart. If you are gardening intensively, you may wish to cut this spacing down considerably, but do not crowd the plants too much or you may also cut down the yield.

Since the seeds gathered from a plant will come true to variety, it makes sense to save seeds from your own crop rather than to buy them each year. Generally speaking, if properly stored, seed will be viable for at least two years. The money you save in this way can be used to buy some exotic variety you haven't yet grown.

Culture

I have always found hot peppers easy to grow and very trouble-free. Since one way organic gardeners get rid of pests is to grind up hot peppers in their blenders and mix them with water to spray on their plants, I guess it is only to be expected that peppers would be free of many of the usual problems.

Good garden practice, such as keeping weeds out, mulching and watering during dry spells and light fertilizing are all that is required. Hot peppers do not require a rich, highly fertile soil and are not heavy feeders.

Harvest

Another nice thing about hot peppers is that they are ready to be picked as soon as the fruit appears. You do not have to wait for them to mature but can pick them green or any other color they turn. Of course you will get more out of a larger pepper because it is larger, and you will also benefit from the fact that mature vegetables develop more vitamins.

When picking peppers, it's best to cut them off rather than pull or break them off. Leave one-half inch of stem so that you do not break the skin of the pepper.

Since the plant will continue to flower and bear fruit, you will have a continual harvest. Ask your market whether they prefer green chilis or hot green or red peppers; they may find one sells better than another. Or you could suggest that they try both and see which sells better.

If you wish to dry the peppers for stringing or just for winter sales, let them mature to the red stage before picking them or they will not dry properly. I just string them up on ordinary sewing thread and hang them in a dry, airy place out of the sun. Later I move a few dried strings to the kitchen, where they look very decorative and are handy to use in cooking.

Be very careful when handling the really hot varieties, and never, never rub your eyes when you have been touching them.

Jerusalem Artichokes (*Helianthus tuberosus*)

Jerusalem artichokes can be found in the produce department of most supermarkets under the name "sunchokes" or "sunflower tubers.'' They usually sell for a dollar or more a pound bag. At this price they are a luxury vegetable, to be used sparingly if at all. The opportunity this presents to the thrifty gardener is enormous; with a little preparation and no care, you can harvest and sell a bountiful crop all year long. And once people have learned the delights of freshly dug Jerusalem artichokes, they will never settle for the travel-weary supermarket version.

The first season I planted Jerusalem artichokes I put them just outside my fenced-in vegetable garden. At the end of the summer I noticed some unfamiliar weeds coming up in that corner. The leaves were similar to the plants growing just outside the fence, and I soon realized some Jerusalem artichokes had escaped into the garden area. I foolishly left them alone, planning to harvest them in the spring before rototilling.

In the spring I carefully dug up all the roots I could find and we had a feast. After rototilling I planted my crops and tended my seedlings. I soon found rototilling had spread the tubers throughout the garden; they were in among the beets, the carrots, the leeks, and the lettuces. Every little bit of root seemed to have sprouted; years later I am still waging war against this wonderful but invasive vegetable. For a lazy gardener who wants to make money, I cannot think of a better choice.

Jerusalem artichokes are very versatile; they are delicious both raw and cooked. Before I go into specifics, however, I want to mention what a boon they are to diabetics and to anyone watching calories. Technically, freshly dug Jerusalem artichokes can be described as 100 percent starch-free. Their carbohydrates are in the form of inulin and levulin, which are approved for diabetic diets. The caloric value of a freshly dug tuber is 7 calories per 100 grams, as compared to 93 for a plain baked potato. The carbohydrate, however, changes as the tuber ages; after long storage the caloric count goes up to 75 per 100 grams and is, therefore, less desirable for special diets. This can be a selling point when talking to health-food stores, which must otherwise rely on a supply ⋅ often grown on the other side of the country. Your garden-fresh Jerusalem artichokes not only taste better, they are actually better for you.

Jerusalem artichokes are so delicious that Europeans have made them a staple of their menus. In England, when first introduced there, they created such a hit that they were made into sweetmeats and sold at a high price to an avid public. Of course, once their free-growing habits made them less exotic, they became, like leeks, a "common" vegetable.

They were introduced on the Continent by the French, who learned of them from the Huron Indians and the Algonquins. In Canada they are sometimes called "artichauts de Canada," but in France they are generally referred to as *topinambour*. The French name is important for gourmet cooks to know, since it is their only clue to recipes for this tuber in books such as *Larousse Gastronomique*, which uses them in recipes for salads, purées, and other dishes. They are also delicious boiled and simply served with butter, and are excellent prepared au gratin, as a vegetable pie, a soufflé, or a soup. And to my way of thinking, they are best when scrubbed and sliced thin, still raw, and added to a salad.

A Note About Preparation:

Do not attempt to peel Jerusalem artichokes before using. Scrub them thoroughly with a vegetable brush and use as is for eating raw or stir-frying. When they are boiled or blanched, their skins will slip off easily and can be removed just before serving.

Appearance

The name "Jerusalem artichoke" has nothing to do with Jerusalem. The origin of the name is not known, but it is supposed to have arisen from the Italian word *girasole*, which means literally "turning to the sun," since the Jerusalem artichoke is a sunflower. As for the rest of the name, it is also not an artichoke, although some people—I among them—think the freshly dug root tastes like globe artichokes.

The plant grows 8 to 12 feet tall, and its blossom is a small sunflower. Some books describe the blossoms as large, but I haven't found this to be so. They are small and so far up (12 feet) that you may easily miss them unless you make a point of checking in the fall.

After a hard frost the stalks are left dry and leafless, like a forest of straight sticks. You will want to remove these (they just snap off) close to ground level, but do not remove them entirely, because they mark the plants and tell you where to dig for the roots. Because of their height, always plant them behind any other sun-loving plants.

The tubers look more like a ginger root than like a potato; they are knobby and awkward to peel (if you should happen to want to). Because of this you will probably prefer to use the larger roots and put the smaller ones back for another season.

When to Plant

If you dig in the garden, you can plant Jerusalem artichokes—spring, summer, fall, and even the middle of the winter if the ground isn't frozen. Consult your own comfort and convenience. The simplest way to start is to ask for a few roots from someone who already grows them (and will be delighted to give some away). If you can't find anyone who grows them, buy a bag from the supermarket. Eat some and plant the rest. Even at a dollar a bag they're a bargain, because you will have soon have more than you can eat from your small planting and will be ready to start getting your money back.

Where to Plant

It is important not only to plant Jerusalem artichokes where their tendency to spread freely doesn't turn them into a pest but also to keep them away from anything else you want to grow. Like sunflower seeds, Jerusalem artichokes are hostile to other plant growth and will stunt anything that grows in their immediate vicinity. If, for instance, you plant them too close to hills of melons, you will soon notice that the hills near the Jerusalem artichokes are looking spindly and unhealthy and you will not get a crop out of that hill.

With those two caveats, you can plant them anywhere you please and that you find convenient. They are not fussy as long as they have full sun. No animals seem to eat the above ground foliage, and, as far as I have noticed, they do not seem to be subject to any pests or diseases.

How to Plant

The tubers have eyes, just like potatoes, and can be cut into several pieces as long as each one has an eye. Prepare your soil by digging down at least a spade's depth. If you're really serious about growing a cash crop, add manure and a little organic fertilizer and mix with the soil in the hole. This vegetable will grow well under conditions of total neglect, but you will get larger tubers and even a greater than usual quantity if you go to some minimal trouble Set them at least a foot apart; they will fill in the spaces between in less than a season. If you plant more than one row, set rows about three feet apart. It won't really matter, because in no time at all, they will be growing all over the place and you will be harvesting as fast as you can. And since this is a book for home gardeners who are just looking for plants with a healthy surplus rather than for commercial garden crops, I really can't imagine your starting out with several rows of this prolific vegetable.

Water or not—they will naturally sprout faster if you start them out with a little moisture—and forget about them. In no time at all you will have strong-looking shoots sprouting well above ground.

Culture

It's entirely up to you and what sort of crop you want. If you baby them a little with ordinary care, the tubers will reward you by being larger and less knobby. The so-called American artichoke (although all Jerusalem artichokes are a native American vegetable) is larger and smoother than other named varieties, but they are not always identified in the store, and a little care will improve whatever strain you have started with.

As with any plants, water and fertilizer are the two important essentials you can control. Since you are interested in the roots rather than in the aboveground product, choose fertilizer low in nitrogen and high in potash and phosphorus.

Jerusalem artichokes will hold their own with almost any weed, but mulching will make digging easier for you and reduce the need for watering. If you mulch well, water during really dry spells, and drop a bit of fertilizer in the ground when you harvest, you will be well rewarded. Or if you want to ignore them completely, except when you dig some for supper, they will do very well on their own and produce incredible amounts of delicious food.

Harvest

An established stand can be harvested from early fall through the winter to late spring. First plantings will mature in about a hundred days. Unlike other root crops, Jerusalem artichokes do not store particularly well and are best when freshly dug. This is another reason why yours will sell better than the ones trucked all the way from California to other states.

When digging for tubers, you will find the largest in a circle about eight inches away from the stalk. You will have to dig deeper than you might expect, so do not settle for the first ones you come upon; there are lots more beneath them. Use a fork spade and just dig up the whole area; you will soon have a bushelbasketful. Leave the rest undisturbed and put back any too small to use. Rake and water the area if you have time, but it isn't strictly necessary.

If you must store the tubers, let them rest in a temperature of about 55 degrees Fahrenheit for about two weeks in a very humid spot. After this period they can be stored in a cool place, at least 40 degrees Fahrenheit but not more than 50. Since this is a lot of trouble, and since they are so easy to dig when wanted, I can't think why you would want to bother storing them. If the market asks, tell them Jerusalem artichokes are handled just like potatoes.

Leeks (*Allium porrum*)

All members of the onion family seem to be universally enjoyed and known, but strangely enough, the leek has never enjoyed the pride of place in America that it has in other countries. I ascribe this, at least in part, to the horrendous price that it commands in the produce department. It seems to me that all of the onion family is meant to be enjoyed in a prodigious manner, and I can easily understand how pricing a couple of leeks at over a dollar dampens any cook's ardor.

In other parts of the world the leek is a common, though respected, vegetable and is eaten in great quantities. It forms the basis for one of the world's great soups, vichyssoise, and is as ubiquitous in Welsh gardens as tomatoes are in ours. In fact, it is the Welsh national emblem—just as the shamrock is the Irish national emblem—and is worn on St. David's Day. Its connection with St. David's Day goes back to A.D. 640, when the Welsh were battling the Saxons. Since it was not possible to distinguish the enemy from themselves by appearance (or, apparently, by uniforms), the Welsh fastened a leek in their headgear, and thus knew that anyone who was not wearing this symbol was a Saxon and the enemy. Since the Welsh won the battle, they gave due credit to the lowly leek and have displayed it at celebrations ever since.

Actually, the leek goes back before recorded history, and its origin or native land is unknown. We do know, however, that it was widely used in Roman times. Nero, who is famous for his musical proclivities, used to eat quantities of leeks because he believed they improved the quality of his singing voice. He ate so many that he was disrespectfully nicknamed Porrophagus; or "leek eater."

Today we know that this excellent vegetable is low in calories and high in valued vitamins and minerals, including vitamin C, potassium, calcium, and phosphorus. In spite of its somewhat coarse appearance, it is mild and delicately flavored when used in cooking.

Leeks are easy to grow, take up comparatively little space, and, if you will take just a little extra trouble, can be harvested year round. They are easy to store and package, and I think you will find them an especially satisfactory cash crop.

Appearance

Leeks look something like scallions in that they grow with white bottoms and green tops. When young they can be eaten like scallions, but that would be very wasteful, since you would be depriving yourself of the mature leek. The green part of the leek, unlike the top of the scallion, is flat and bladelike, and the color is somewhat gray-green rather than the brilliant emerald of the scallion.

Leeks differ from scallions also in that they must be blanched if you wish the white part to be white. Since blanching them tends to make them sandy (due to the method used), some gardeners prefer to grow them without covering them. I cannot comment on this because I have never had the courage to risk a crop of leeks by letting them grow au naturel. If you are growing a lot, you might like to try this method, but I would not recommend it for leeks you plan to market.

When to Plant

Leeks are not delicate and can be planted in fairly cold weather, as soon as the ground can be worked. You can plant another crop in July and mulch this for use all winter. As long as you keep the leeks (and the ground) from freezing, you will be able to dig down through the snow, move aside the mulch, and gather at your pleasure.

If you wish an early spring crop, start the seeds indoors in flats. Leeks transplant easily and will command higher prices in the market if you beat the season.

Where to Plant

Leeks can be planted anywhere you please as long as the soil is reasonably fertile, well-watered, and free of clods, rocks, and roots. Animals will not eat them and they have few insect enemies. If you find them especially attractive, as some gardeners do, you might put them in the flower bed, where they may help deter pests.

How to Plant

First dig a ditch. This is not so arduous as it sounds, since it needn't be a very big ditch. Just hoe out a narrow ditch about 4 inches deep. Mix in a generous portion of well-rotted manure combined with soil until the ditch is about 2 inches deep. Then sow seeds shallowly, about one-quarter inch deep.

Be patient. The seeds will take about two weeks to germinate, and as you water to keep the soil moist, the weeds will try to take over. It is important to keep the ditch well weeded for most of the growing season or the weeds will soon be impossible to remove without disturbing the slender, chivelike shoots of the young leek seedlings.

When the seedlings are about 3 inches high, thin them to stand about 6 inches apart. Don't throw away the seedlings; they are easily transplanted to another ditch.

Culture

Leeks require no special care other than weeding and watering. A bead of 10–10–10 fertilizer in mid-season would be welcome but is not absolutely necessary if your garden is reasonably fertile.

As the leeks grow, fill in the ditch with earth so that the white part will be blanched—that is to say, so that it will stay white. This should be done gradually until finally the two inches of the bottom part of the leek are underground.

Harvest

This is a good crop for the impatient gardener since leeks can be harvested over a very long period. The first leeks can be gathered when an inch and a half or more in diameter and the last can be taken in late autumn—unless you plan to leave them in the ground over the winter. Naturally, the longer you let them grow, the bigger they will become. Large leeks, as big around as a man's thumb, bring a better price in the market and are more useful for dishes that call for braising.

If you wish to gather leeks and store them, do not gather them until they are mature; the flat tops will fan out and sort of flop over, but do not wait for them to turn brown, as you do with onions. The best way to judge a mature leek is to look for the stubby thickness of the bottom half and consider the length of time that has elapsed since planting.

When marketing leeks you might want to add a personal touch by including a suggestion for removing the sand from them. Because the earth is pulled up around them as they grow, a certain amount is liable to find its way between the layers of the white section. This is easily removed by cutting the leek in halves or quarters (depending on the thickness and your recipe) the long way and carefully separating the layers lightly with your fingers under running water. The sand will easily wash out.

Luffa (*Luffa cylindrica*)

Luffa is an edible gourd, but for the gardener interested in a cash crop its chief use is as a material for making a number of useful items. Among the things that can be made are dishcloths, bathroom sponges, pillow and mattress stuffing, strainers, door- and bathmats, sandals, sun helmets, potholders, and car-washing sponges. You may already be familiar with the loofah sponges sold in drugstores. They come in an assortment of sizes and are usually packed in a clear plastic bag and displayed in bins. A loofah bathroom sponge is especially good because it is not only very pleasant to use but also never seems to mold or to react in any other unpleasant way to bathroom moisture. I have had one in my bathroom for over three years and use it at least once a day; it is still just as fresh and agreeable as the day I processed it from my garden. With the shortage and high price of sea sponges, a vegetable sponge from the garden should prove a welcome substitute and have a ready market. You have an advantage over commercial producers because you can sell your products much less expensively and still make a good profit.

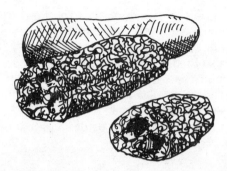

Luffa is actually superior for many of these uses to more commonly used products. The U.S. Navy, for instance, preferred luffa filters for their steam engines, although price was no object and they could have used any other material. When used for stuffing pillows and mattresses, it is very cool and does not give off a damp odor during humid weather. Only your own ingenuity and craft ability limit what you can do with luffa. If you are not very creative in this area, you can still make the sponges in no time at all.

Of course the bonus in luffa is that the young fruit is also good to eat—prepared in any way you would use zucchini, including sliced raw. In addition, the young leaves and flowers are a welcome, if somewhat unusual, addition to your table.

Not all seed catalogs list luffa but many do. The only difficulty is the detective work involved in tracking down the nomenclature the seedsman has used. Thompson & Morgan, for example, lists it under flowers as "luffa" and heads the text in the body of the catalog "Grow your own bathroom sponge." Hudson calls it Dish Cloth Gourd, Park lists it under flowers as Dishrag Gourd and Nichols calls it Japanese Bottle Luffa. As you can see, it can be found in a wide range of catalogs, but it may take a bit of hunting to ferret it out.

Appearance

Luffa is a vine that grows rampantly. It is best trained on a fence, where it can twine as far around the garden as it pleases without taking up valuable in-ground space. The flowers and leaves are typical of gourds and both are edible when gathered young—in fact, the flower buds are especially tasty.

The fruit also is edible but only when very young. To prepare it for eating, do not peel it but do pare off the ridges. If you are into Chinese cooking, you may run across recipes for luffa under the name "Chinese okra." The name has to do with the appearance of the fruit, not its taste, so do not be discouraged from trying it just because you dislike okra.

When to Plant

Luffa is very frost-sensitive and cannot be planted until all danger of frost has passed and the ground has warmed up thoroughly. Since it takes 115 days to maturity, you may have to start it indoors in your area; if so, start it in March or April (count back from your earliest fall frost date). Peat pots are the simplest medium and will prevent the seedlings from being set back when you put them in the ground. Two seeds to a pot, thinned to one if they both germinate, are about all you will be able to fit in. Do not hesitate to grow luffa just because of its warmth requirement. Johnny's Selected Seeds, which is in Maine, both lists luffa in its catalog and grows luffa in its Maine garden.

Where to Plant

As I have mentioned, luffa takes up a lot of room and is best grown on a fence in full sun. The vine may easily grow over the fence and into the meadow, but that is no problem so long as the area around the roots are kept weed-free and fertilized and watered on schedule.

How to Plant

Seeds are large and easy to handle. Before sowing, prepare the soil by digging in well-rotted manure and 10–10–10 fertilizer in the rows or hills. Cover with at least an inch of garden soil and sow the seeds 1 inch deep. If you like to plant in hills, the seeds should be 3 inches apart and the hills 6 feet apart; if in rows, plant the seeds 4 inches apart in rows 4 feet apart. I cheat and plant in rows much closer together because I feel the fencing allows me to. Incidentally, another advantage of growing luffa up a fence is that it keeps the fruit off the ground. Otherwise, put black plastic underneath the fruit as it forms so that it doesn't rot.

Once you have planted the seed—whether indoors or out—keep the ground moist until the seedlings appear. This may require a bit of patience, since the seeds are slow to germinate and may take as long as two weeks. You can sometimes speed things up by covering the seeded areas with black plastic during the cooler night temperatures. Just be sure not to leave it on once the seedlings have broken through the ground.

Culture

Luffa is a heavy feeder and requires fertilizing about every three weeks. A high-nitrogen fertilizer plus a side-dressing of manure gives the best crop. If you have a good compost pile, this will do equally well. Frequent and deep watering is also important, since, like all gourds and squashes, luffa is a very thirsty plant.

There are not many pests to worry about, but keep an eye out for borer and take the usual precautions. If they do get into the vine, treat it as you would zucchini.

Harvest

If you wish to eat the leaves and flower buds, gather them when the vines are still young. The fruit should be picked when immature, not more than 4 to 6 inches long. It tastes something like English peas and, like zucchini, does not need to be peeled. It is advisable, however, to remove the ridges with a vegetable parer. Luffa can be eaten raw like cucumbers or cooked like zucchini. If you would like to experiment, dry the young fruit. It is considered a culinary delicacy by the Chinese and will keep indefinitely if properly stored.

The seeds—and there are hundreds of them—can be dried and eaten like pumpkin or sunflower seeds; they make a most unusual and delicious cocktail snack.

To prepare the gourd for use as sponges or for making the various other articles we have discussed, allow the fruit to mature on the vine. When it is ripe, pick and store it—being careful not to let one fruit touch another—in a dry place. It is all right to put the fruit in the sun if you take it in at night so the dew will not touch it. After a few days cut off the ends and shake out the seeds. If they do not shake out easily, leave the gourds to dry longer. Be sure to save the seeds even if you do not wish to eat them; you will never have to buy luffa seeds again.

The next step is to soak off the skin, and this is done by immersing the gourds in hot water until it can be peeled off. This may take a few days, in which case you will have to change the water and add fresh hot water. Once you have peeled off all the skin and removed any seeds that may remain, put the sponges aside to dry thoroughly. They will look something like long bars of shredded wheat and, depending on your crop, may grow as large as 2 feet long and 4 inches in diameter. This is the basic sponge, which can be packaged and sold without further ado. All other products are made from this.

Raspberries (*Rubus*)

All berries make good cash crops, but since raspberries sell for the most money, they make the best cash crop of all. They are no more difficult to grow or less prolific than other berries; the only reason they are more expensive to buy in the market is that they are too fragile to withstand the rigors of modern distribution methods. And, unlike the tomato, which has been developed into new varieties that have the hardiness and taste of tennis balls, the raspberry has stubbornly refused to yield its delicious nature to the exigencies of modern marketing.

Anyone who doesn't grow raspberries must look upon them as a luxury. In spite of this, raspberries have never lost their popularity and can be found in the frozen-food section along with strawberries and blueberries—only in smaller packages and in heavy syrup. If you have a small raspberry patch you can dine like royalty on however many raspberries take your fancy and still have enough to market.

There are many varieties of raspberries: they come red, black, purple, yellow, and gold. They can be everbearing or bear once or twice a season, depending on your stock. One thing is sure, once you have planted raspberries, you will never have to buy a plant again unless you wish to try a different variety from the ones you are already growing. I happen to prefer red raspberries, although the black ones—sometimes called blackcaps—have their own delicious raspberry flavor, and there are growers who think only the yellow are worth their time.

Where to Plant

It's possible to plant raspberries in a vegetable garden, but I advise against it. For one thing, they should not be planted in soil that has recently grown eggplants, peppers, tomatoes, or potatoes. For another, they sucker so freely that they interfere with other crops, and often the suckers have gotten a toehold before you realize it. If this happens in the middle of the lettuce or cress bed, it is most inconvenient. Another reason to keep them out of the vegetable bed is that they are bramble fruits and, therefore, prickly. Backing into a raspberry bush when you are merely trying to pick a few zucchini is not the greatest way to start the dinner hour. Ideally a raspberry bed should be devoted to raspberries. It doesn't need to be very large, and it doesn't need to get out of hand, like a wild raspberry patch. A nice, neat rectangle in a sunny spot in the lawn is perfectly workable.

When to Plant

Raspberry roots are usually shipped in the spring when it is time to set them out in your area. Get your order in early so that the stock is not shipped late or the plants may suffer too great a shock when uprooted for transplanting.

How to Plant

Ideally the soil should be prepared before the roots arrive. The best way is to dig up the area where you plan to set out the plants and mix the soil thoroughly with wood ashes, well-rotted manure and a lot of compost. Since a sandy or gravelly soil that is rich in humus is the best kind, the nearer you can come to these conditions, the better your crop will be. In any case the soil should be friable and the area should drain well. Be sure the site is airy—not in a hollow where there is comparatively little air movement. It is not necessary to dig down as deeply as for asparagus or for root vegetables—about 6 inches deep is sufficient—but this is a permanent planting, so a little extra effort in ensuring the fertility of the soil is well worth while.

When you receive the roots, do not unwrap them until just before you intend to plant. They should be soaked in warm water for about two hours before setting in the ground, but they will rot if left in water too long. On the other hand, they must never dry out, which they will do if you unwrap them and leave them in the open air for any length of time. If they arrive at an inconvenient time, unwrap them, soak them for a couple of hours, and heel them in until you are ready to plant them. Even with this treatment, the sooner they are set in their bed, the better.

Canes should be set 3 to 4 feet apart, and this distance should be maintained in the years to come as the roots sucker. Rows should be 6 to 7 feet apart, and the size of the bed depends entirely on how many plants you want. If the raspberries have their own bed, try to site it where it can be enlarged later on when you have discovered the joys of raising your own fruit. Most nurseries include planting instructions with the shipment, and these will tell you whether or not the canes require any additional pruning (they will have been pruned when dug at the nursery).

A word about varieties. Trying to choose varieties from the catalog is very unsatisfactory, because the writers of garden catalogs make each variety sound more desirable than the one before it. There is one characteristic to look for, and do not order a variety that does not have it no matter how great it sounds. It must be virus-free. Raspberries are subject to certain pests and diseases, and a "virus-free" assurance in the description will free you from one of the most trying of them.

To plant the presoaked roots, dig a hole deep enough so that they can be set in with the buds facing upward. Handle the roots gently to avoid injuring the buds. The stalk should be vertical, so it may be necessary to dig a somewhat horizontal hole to accommodate the bottom part of the cane. When the hole is half full, water it thoroughly, and then fill in the rest of the soil to ground level. Do not tamp down the top half of the soil too firmly or you will make it difficult for the buds to break through. Keep the soil fairly moist until the canes start to show signs of growth and the buds are active.

Once the canes and roots are in place, keep the area free of weeds. As soon as blossoms appear you can mulch heavily with compost, wood chips, straw, or something similar. The purpose of the early mulching is to retain moisture and to keep down the weeds. Once the canes have fruited, remove or dig in some of the mulch so that it is not quite so thick; new shoots will be coming up to form the basis for next year's crop, and a too heavy mulch will discourage not only weeds but the shoots as well. At this point you will have to go back to clean cultivation, being careful not to disturb new raspberry growth.

While red raspberries will sucker and thus provide an eternal supply of new canes, black raspberries will propagate themselves by tip-layering. As the canes grow long, toward the end of the summer, they will arch over and eventually touch the ground, and where they touch they will root. You can control this process by pinching back the canes so that they do not grow so long or you can direct the tips to the area where you want new plants. If you want to give nature a hand, bury the tip a couple of inches in the soil and firm the ground around it. Water it occasionally, and, once you are fairly sure it has rooted, separate it from the parent plant with clippers. Often black raspberries will also sucker, but tip-rooting is the usual method of propagating these varieties. If you have all the plants you want in that bed, it is easy to dig up the rooted tip and transplant it where you want it to grow.

Disease

The trouble with raspberry diseases is that they are almost inevitable. There are, however, preventive measures to take and ways of controlling problems once they arise. The most important preventive measure is clean culture. This includes removal of old canes and diseased plants. All discarded material should be burned and never added to the compost heap. If the infestation has been so bad that you have to replant the bed, do not plant in the same area as before for several years. Choose only virus-free or virus-resistant varieties. Do not plant varieties together; for instance, do not mix black and red raspberries in the same bed. Examine the plants from time to time and remove any egg clusters from both the tops and the bottoms of the leaves. If the leaves look odd, remove and burn them. Some problems, such as rust, will probably always occur in some degree but are rarely serious. Occasionally the plants may be infested with borers; these should be cut out, just as when they occur in squash vines.

Culture

Raspberries, like roses, require clean culture. If you allow weeds to take hold, you will have more problems with disease and pests and will find it very difficult to get rid of the weeds without disturbing the canes and getting thoroughly scratched. Weeds will also make it more difficult to prune, and this is a very important part of raspberry culture.

Pruning makes the difference between a wild, neglected patch of raspberries and a high-yielding cultivated bed. The rules differ slightly according to the type and variety. For instance, red raspberries, except for the everbearing, are pruned differently from black or purple.

To prune any variety of the everbearing type, cut them back after the first summer crop instead of waiting until after the fall crop. To prune red and yellow raspberries that are not everbearing, prune only in the fall by taking out all the canes that have fruited. If you have too many canes in the spring, it is all right to remove some of the weaker ones, and of course you must always remove the suckers you do not want and transplant those you do, whenever you spot them.

Black and purple varieties should be pinched off at the tips as soon as the new shoots are about 2 to 3 feet tall. All varieties, once they have fruited, should have all the fruiting canes disposed of— they will not bear again and only take up room in the bed—and the others cut back to about 8 inches long. If there are lateral branches, these should be cut back also.

In addition to already fruited canes (which will die out if not removed and crowd the bed unproductively), laterals, and weak canes, any diseased canes should be removed as soon as they are detected. If this is not done, the disease will quickly spread through the whole bed and your only recourse will be to start from scratch with fresh plant material.

All new shoots should be topped each summer when they are 2 or 3 feet high; no canes should be allowed to reach more than 6 feet until you are tip-layering. This may puzzle you if you are familiar with an old, neglected patch that covers a quarter of an acre and has not been pruned for years. The difference in yield with a properly pruned patch will soon convince you that it is worth the time; if you are using the surplus for a cash crop, you will be well rewarded for your labor.

Harvest

No one will have to tell you when the berries are ripe—the birds and the squirrels will announce the event a couple of days before it happens. At this point a cover of netting is necessary or you will lose as much as you gather. Squirrels are not easily deterred, but a few bells hung from the bushes, near the ground and under the netting, will make them nervous. Woodchucks sometimes take to the bushes and may even pull down branches to feed from them. If you can figure out what to do about this, I would love to hear from you. But no matter how many wild friends you must share your crop with, there will still be enough for all (with netting) if you bear in mind that early-morning harvesting will help you get your fair share. When the berries are at their peak I pick twice a day so as to chase the birds and get as many berries as possible as they ripen.

As soon as the berries are gathered they should be packaged in trays and taken to the market. You can alert your stores with a phone call, but they will be receptive whenever the crop is ready. Since raspberries are so fragile, it is best to handle them as little as possible (never wash them before packing them) and to get them to the market as soon as possible. They will not linger long in the produce department, but if by any chance they do, it is better if they are as fresh as possible, so that they will last until they are sold.

Sell only firm berries; never sell wet or overripe ones. These are best kept for your own use or turned into vinegar or a tasty drink and marketed in this form. An old-fashioned raspberry drink that is very refreshing on a hot summer day can be made with a three-to-one mixture of raspberries and vinegar that is brewed for three days and then put in a jelly bag to squeeze and drain. Add sugar to taste (about a pound to a pint), boil for a minute or two to dissolve, and blend. Cool and bottle. Just one inch of this concoction in a glass of ice water, with or without a jigger of an alcoholic beverage, makes an unusual and delicious drink.

Rhubarb (*Rheum rhaponticum*)

Rhubarb is one of the vegetables—like leeks—that were once common as dirt and now bring high prices in the market. Not so long ago no home was complete without a bed of rhubarb growing by the kitchen door. It deserves to be more popular with home gardeners since it is easy to raise, makes delicious eating, is good for you (don't tell the kids), and can be a money-making crop for the small garden.

Hint:

Rhubarb will sell best early in the spring and again when strawberries are in season. To be ready for spring selling, take the time to force some; to coordinate with the strawberry season, watch your local market for reasonably priced berries, which will appear long before the natives are ripe.

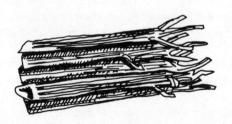

A native of Siberia, rhubarb arrived in the West through Russia by way of China. Camel caravans carried it as far as Greece and Rome. Its refreshingly tart taste, sweetened with a bit of honey, was a welcome spring tonic after a long winter, and American colonists valued it as a vegetable that could be eaten as a fruit.

Rhubarb's old-fashioned name, "pie plant," tells you its most popular culinary use. It is also delicious stewed. It is often combined with strawberries because their sweetness offsets the tartness; otherwise honey performs the same function. There are many variations on these two basics—fruit combinations, old-fashioned desserts of all sorts, and even a rhubarb wine. I have never tasted this last concoction and famous gourmet author André Simon thought it not worth the trouble.

Do not hesitate to serve stewed rhubarb as an accompaniment to a roast or to a cold-meat platter. And remember, it contains vitamins A and C and calcium, as well as other nutrients.

Appearance

Rhubarb stalks are a beautiful pink-red. If they are too pale or on the green side, the plants are probably not getting enough sun. The leaves are very attractive—slightly crinkled, dark green, glossy, and quite large, so that they form a compact mass in their area.

When to Plant

Rhubarb can be planted both spring and fall—or any time you find it convenient, depending on whether you are planting roots or dividing a clump. It can be started from seed, but this is not recommended. For one thing, it will then take forever to reach sufficient age for a good harvest; for another, the seedlings will not come true. It is far easier to plant two- or three-year-old roots from the nursery. If you plant in the early spring, the soil will be in an ideal condition but you will not have a crop until the following spring. If you plant three-year roots in the fall, you can harvest in the spring.

If you get roots from a neighbor who is dividing his clumps, plant them right away or sprinkle with water and cover them with damp peat moss. If you order them from a seedsman, plant within three days of receiving them and do not open the package until you have the hole dug and ready or the roots will dry out and die. This is the only time rhubarb is at all delicate.

The seedsman will send you proper roots, but if you get them from a friend, be sure each root division contains at least one healthy-looking (not dried-out) bud or eye. If you know a fellow gardener with a mature clump, do not hesitate to ask for some; you will be doing him or her a favor and helping to keep your donor's bed producing at its maximum.

How to Plant

Since rhubarb is a perennial and will stay in place for a number of years, it is important to put in sufficient time preparing the soil in which it will grow. Rhubarb is generally planted in hills, but the planting hole should be deep and wide, well spaded to 12 to 16 inches. The hole should then be filled with a rich mixture of well-rotted manure, wood ashes, and 10–10–10 fertilizer plus an application of nitrate of soda. If rabbit or chicken manure, rather than horse, is used, the higher nitrogen content will give spectacular results.

The roots should be set 3 to 5 inches deep, with an eye or bud pointing upward. Leave about 3 feet between plants in every direction; the leaves will soon form a compact mass and shade the ground, helping to keep down weed growth.

Culture

Rhubarb is a very heavy feeder and will respond if kept well watered and well fed. It prefers cool, moist summers, and the only way to grow it successfully during hot summers is with frequent watering and heavy mulch. On the whole, however, rhubarb is undemanding and will grow without that extra bit of coddling, but not quite as well. It is basically considered a plant that is not at all finicky and that will grow anywhere practically forever. It is often found in gardens of old houses that have been abandoned.

In the spring and fall topdress it with about a foot of well-rotted manure. In the spring lightly cultivate in this mulch and leave it in place for an earlier crop. Keep the bed weed-free (not too much of a problem if planted closely) or the weeds will compete for the fertilizer and take it away from the rhubarb plants.

Harvest

The tender shoots of early spring are the sweetest. They can be brought on quite early by forcing if you wish to get into the markets early. To force your plants, place a box, small barrel, or similar container, with top and bottom removed, over the clump. If you then put a piece of glass or plastic over the top, the sun will warm up the air inside and the plant will begin to grow, trying to reach the sun and encouraged by the warmth. Glass will generally create more interior warmth than plastic, but both work. If you want to force even faster, or earlier, use a wooden container (such as the small barrel) and surround it with about a foot and a half of fresh—not rotted—manure. Fresh manure generates a surprising amount of heat, and that will add to the heat from the sun and speed things up, sometimes as much as two weeks, because you can start while the weather is still quite cold.

It is important not to harvest until the plants are sufficiently mature. One-year-old plants should not be harvested at all. Two-year plants may be harvested lightly. Three-year plants are mature and can be heavily harvested. Obviously, if you want quick results, you should buy at least two-year roots; the older they are, the more the seedsman will charge for them. If you get them from a neighbor's clump, remember to ask how old they are.

When you try to plan the quantity you will get from your bed, you will find that estimates vary. This is understandable, because it is not a crop most people eat regularly, so it is difficult to predict how much any one family might eat. You could start out with 8 plants and see how much of a surplus that gives you. On the other hand, even 3 or 4 plants might leave some to sell in a family that is content with one rhubarb pie a season. You will just have to see for yourself.

Important Note:

When harvesting, do not cut the stalks; they should be pulled off. You will find this is easy and does not uproot the plant. Also, never eat the leaves; cut them off. The leaves are poisonous because they have a very high calcium oxalate content.

As a clump becomes old and crowded, the stalks will become slender and not so profuse. This is a sign that you need to dig up the clump, cut it apart into eye-bearing roots, and replant. If you wish to keep harvesting the maximum amount, divide your clumps before this happens. Unfortunately, only experience will tell you how often this needs to be done. Some experts will say clumps should be divided every five years; others say a clump can be undisturbed for twenty-five years; and those in between advise dividing every eight or nine years. Obviously, where the clumps are growing and under what conditions have some affect on how long they remain productive. I think the only way you can know for sure—and no one wants to divide a clump if it doesn't need it—is to wait for the first signs of lessening yield. Then check your records for how many years it has been since it was planted, and make a note to divide your clumps a year earlier than that from then on.

Pests and Diseases

Rhubarb is fairly free from pests and diseases, providing it is fed and watered to its liking. Occasionally, however, you may run into some problems. These are the most common:

Borers are not nearly as frequent in rhubarb as in zucchini. If you should get an infestation, the treatment is the same: cut out the borer with a knife. The other stalks will be fine, and you may even be able to salvage part of the stalk the borer has been eating.

Leaf insects will sometimes be attracted to rhubarb, but they are usually the sort that can be controlled with a little systematic hand-picking when they first appear.

Scallions (*Allium fistulosum*)

All members of the onion family have been popular since the dawn of history. This is no exaggeration, since onions have been found with Bronze Age artifacts and have been a staple of man's diet down through the ages. The Egyptians credited a diet of onions, garlic, and radishes with furnishing their slaves the strength to build the pyramids, and the Romans fed onions to their soldiers to help conquer the lands that made up their empire.

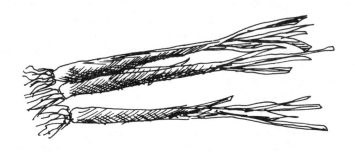

In addition to its contribution to the culinary arts, therefore, the onion family has long been credited with beneficial medicinal qualities. An onion a day was recommended long before apples as contributing to longevity, and onions were used to fight chest infections and high blood pressure and to promote the healing of burns (when applied as poultices). As with many folkloric remedies that modern man came to scoff at, the efficacy of onions has been vindicated by modern science. As it turns out, onions contain an antibiotic, as well as a number of other beneficial ingredients. Since the odor of raw onions can be readily dissipated by eating parsley, and since their flavor, both cooked and raw, adds zest to so many dishes, they will undoubtedly be in demand for a long time to come.

Scallions, a member of the onion family, are also one of the most popular. They used to be called spring onions because they were available primarily in the spring. Now, however, we can grow them over a long season, and they are an easy crop for the home gardener to supply to local markets.

You will almost never find "scallions" listed as such in seed catalogs. To get your starter crop, look under "onions," "bunching onions," "Welsh onions," "multiplier onions," or "green onions." In spite of this wealth of nomenclature, there are really only three kinds of scallions—and even then only two of them are true scallions.

The scallions that are not considered true scallions are the immature onions that are produced by onion sets. Onion sets are small immature onions that are sold in the spring in garden shops from small bins. They are usually sold by the pound and are not distinguished by variety, although they may vary in color. This is an expensive way to grow scallions, since it means you are cropping early at the expense of a mature onion. Most home gardeners do not know there is any other way to grow scallions, so they always use some of their regular onion crop this way in order to get this delectable vegetable. There is, however, a way to have your scallions and your onions too.

Instead of buying onion sets, the home gardener who hopes to realize a cash crop (and also less expensive scallions for the kitchen) should grow scallions from bunching, multiplier, or Welsh onions. All of these will produce scallions that have straight tips without little bulbs on the end. True scallions are grown from seed, and an initial planting will keep on growing year after year forever. Unlike onions, true scallions will never form bulbs and can be harvested over a long period. They require very little work after the first season and will be available from early spring until a really hard frost (and even longer if you mulch the clumps). Once you have tried true scallions you will never again use onion sets for anything but onions.

Appearance

In the beginning, scallions look like onion sprouts; each slender green thread forms from a seed and looks much too delicate to survive into maturity. Their delicate appearance is deceptive; the seedlings can be transplanted with relative impunity if the need should ever arise.

As they grow, each seed develops clumps, or bunches—hence the name "bunching onion" or "multiplier onion" (because it multiplies). I cannot give you an equally logical explanation for the name "Welsh onion"; although very popular in Wales and grown extensively in Welsh gardens, it has nothing to do with that country and did not originate there.

The appearance of the scallions that grow from these seeds is exactly what you would expect a scallion to look like—unless you mistakenly think that scallions should have a small bulb on the end. If you remember that only the so-called scallions, or green onions grown from onion seeds or onion sets, have a bulb, you will be able to distinguish between them in the supermarket and can impress your less knowledgeable friends by pointing out this distinction.

When to Plant

Scallions like cool weather; they are not even deterred by light frosts. So as soon as you can get at the garden, you can plant scallion seeds. The clumps will be permanent (if you want them to be), and this means that a planting may interfere if put in an area of the garden that is regularly rototilled. They can, however, be moved when necessary and should be divided, in any case, fairly regularly. The mature clump is quite handsome and would not be out of place in the herb or flower garden. The flowers are attractive and always full of bees—which is useful to know when you have some crops or plants that are often not satisfactorily pollinated.

Where to Plant

Since rabbits, woodchucks, and other animals will not eat any member of the onion family, including scallions, it is not necessary to put them in a fenced-in garden. They do require full sun and a fairly rich, well-dug area, free of rocks, large stones, roots, and clods. With these limitations in mind, plus the fact that they should be a more or less permanent planting, you can plant them wherever it is convenient.

Like all members of the onion family, they are said to deter aphids and other insect pests, so they might be beneficial if planted between roses and other flowers that would otherwise require special care. They do not, however, get along favorably with peas and beans and should never be planted with them.

How to Plant

The seeds are tiny and therefore a little hard to handle. Before sowing, dig the earth up in the row and incorporate a good quantity of well-rotted manure and wood ashes, as well as a 10–10–10 fertilizer. Scallions are more sensitive to acid soil than many other vegetables and the wood ashes will help keep the pH on the alkaline side. If you have trouble growing them successfully, you may need to add lime in the fall. Be sure the materials are well mixed into the soil, and then firm it well before planting the seeds one-half inch deep. All onions require a firm seedbed because their roots are shallow, and until they take hold, they will not do well in a loose soil.

Allow ten inches between plants. As the clumps mature, you can dig them up and space them farther apart if you wish.

Culture

The culture requirement of scallions can be summed up in one verb: "weed." Weeds will quickly outgrow the slender seedlings and will be almost impossible to remove without disturbing the new roots. It is absolutely essential to keep the seedbed clear of all weeds, and the only way to do this is to pull up the weeds while they are still tiny. I find the weeding is best done by hand, although some gardeners claim they can run a hand fork down the row, guiding the seedlings into one of the areas between the tines and digging down ever so slightly to dislodge the weeds on either side. While the theory sounds good, I find that in practice some weeds will grow so close to the seedlings that you practically need a magnifying glass to see which shoot to grasp. And careful though I try to be, I invariably, sooner or later, come up with a clump of weeds from which one scallion seedling reproachfully waves. If you neglect weeding for any length of time, pulling up the weeds will disturb the roots of the scallions, which will need to be pressed back into the soil and watered for comfort. Your only consolation is that weeding at such an early stage is not onerous and can be done with a coffee cup in one hand while you are finishing breakfast.

Some garden books recommend seeding at three-week intervals, but I have never found it necessary, because I keep harvesting the clumps and they continue to grow. If, however, you need a larger crop to satisfy all your customers, you can seed every three weeks until the really hot weather starts. Then give yourself a few weeks off and start again for a fall crop.

Watering should be done whenever there is a dry spell, but scallions do not require as much water as most other vegetables. Additional fertilizing with a 5–10–10 mixture can be done during the growing season, especially if you feel the plants are not coming along as fast as they should.

Harvest

The first scallions will be ready to pick in about 60 days—even sooner if you don't mind some fairly slender ones. Harvesting can continue from then on. They will theoretically mature in about 120 days, but if you have continually harvested the clump, new scallions will keep coming. I always have more than I can use, so my clumps increase in size each year and my problem is getting enough slender scallions. This is the only reason I can think of that you might want to reseed; the smaller scallions may sell better in the market.

If you decide you want to reseed a couple of times a season, let the flowers go to seed and gather the heads before the seeds fall. The clump will reseed itself but not necessarily where and how you want it to, so it is best to control this aspect yourself. Put the seed-heads in an open paper bag and leave them in a dry place for a week or so. Then shake the heads into the bag and gather up the seed to save for the next season. You will find seed production is very prolific; you will never need to buy seed no matter how large a planting you decide on.

Scallions are not a vegetable you can store. They must be gathered shortly before using or selling. Because of their long season, this is no problem. It will take a sharp frost, one that really makes the ground hard, to deter scallion growth, and with a deep mulch, you can even harvest in the snow.

In marketing your scallions, you might want to take advantage of the fact that yours are true scallions and home-grown to boot. An easy and attractive way to make this known would be to tie your scallion bunches with some distinctive kind of tie (colored cord, for example) and add a small tag (cut from inexpensive poster board or oaktag) with your name and a note about their being real, genuine scallions.

Shallots (*Allium ascalonicum*)

Shallots are a member of the onion family but are even easier to grow. On the other hand, unlike the onion, which is thought of as a plebian vegetable, shallots are the darling of haute cuisine and beloved of cooks everywhere. Since, in addition, shallots are usually prohibitively expensive in the produce department, they lend themselves very naturally to our cash-crops category. And they are ideal for the small garden because they take up very little room.

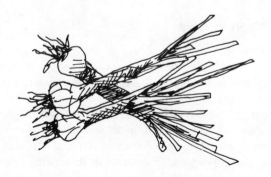

Historically, shallots are an ancient vegetable. The Romans knew of and valued them and they were written about by Pliny. Chefs in the time of Charlemagne used them to create their classic recipes, which we still use today.

The beauty of shallots is their ability to lend an oniony flavor to a dish but with a delicacy that we do not usually associate with this family. Once you have used shallots, you will come to depend on them. In marketing them to the public, you might increase sales by including a simple, classic recipe; often someone will avoid buying an unfamiliar vegetable simply because of not knowing how to use it. With the price you will get for your shallots, you can well afford to offer a little literature that will increase their use.

Appearance

Shallots look very much like garlic except that they are smaller and have brown, rather than white, skins. You will find them in the produce department of most supermarkets, usually packed in small trays, several to a package. If you do not see any, ask the department manager whether they are out of season or simply not stocked by that store. They are usually easy to find.

When to Plant

Set shallots out in early spring as soon as the ground can be worked. They will usually take the whole season to form and mature. It is possible to leave any extras to overwinter, in which case they will start growing again in the spring. This is not always successful, unless you would like some early shoots to use as shallot-flavored chives—a tasty addition to an early spring salad but not very useful as a cash crop.

Shallots can be ordered through your seed catalog, but I usually buy a batch at the market, just as with garlic. Each shallot contains numerous cloves, and each of these is planted separately, so before buying your original stock, figure out how large an area you want to devote to shallots.

Of course, when you get really started, you will be able to save part of each year's crop to plant for the next season. With this system you will never again need to purchase sets for planting—an obvious savings in addition to the cash you will realize from selling part of your crop. Do not, however, try to save shallot cloves more than one season; they will dry out and will be neither edible nor plantable.

Where to Plant

Shallots do not like a soil that is heavy and clayey or too sandy. For best results, pick a site that is moderately well drained (although this is not as critical as with some other vegetables) and rich and loamy. If you want to go in for shallots in a big way, it might be worthwhile to prepare the soil the season before you plan to plant. This will allow you to dig in compost and well-rotted manure and bring the soil up to its ideal condition. With organic gardening methods it takes a little longer to develop full fertility, so add organic fertilizer the season before planting and mix it well with the soil. You will still want to fertilize when planting and during the growing season, but fertilizing the previous season will give the soil bacteria time to do their work and create a rich, fertile bed for your shallots. If all this sounds like too much work, however, you will still get good results preparing, fertilizing, and planting all in the early spring, unless your soil is really poor.

Shallots require full sun and an area free of roots, rocks, and anything else that would interfere with root development.

How to Plant

Allow 2 to 3 inches between cloves and 10 to 16 inches between rows.

Each head should be carefully divided into cloves without damaging them and without scraping off the protective skin. When you are choosing cloves from your crop to use for planting, save the bigger ones to use in cooking and plant the smaller ones. In the beginning, however, you may wish to plant all of them in order to reduce the number of heads you have to buy. If the price of purchase is based on weight, choose small heads and you will get a greater number of cloves for your money.

Make a hole about one inch deep with a pencil or dibber and put the clove in with the narrow, pointy end up. Firm the soil over the cloves and water if you wish to start them growing right away. In planting, discard any cloves that are brown-colored or feel papery when gently pressed between your fingers.

If you wish to get maximum use out of your space, take advantage of the long growing season of shallots to plant some earlier crops along with them. For instance, you can plant lettuce, garden cress, spinach, or any other leafy, low-growing vegetable in between. Such crops will be harvested and out of the way long before the shallots need the extra room. Do not plant root vegetables, however, in that space.

You will get best results with fertilizer that is high in phosphorus and potash. If you have a general vegetable mixture that you use, add the additional phosphorus and potash separately at the same time as the regular fertilizer. Or mix a small amount of the two together and store especially for your root vegetables.

Shallots are more sensitive than many other vegetables to a soil that is somewhat acid. If you have reason to suspect that your soil is acid, or if you have not limed for several growing seasons, it is advisable to add finely pulverized lime the season before you plan to set out shallots.

Culture

Regular watering is necessary to keep the shallots growing. If at any point lack of water causes them to stop growing, you will not have a satisfactory crop. It is necessary, of course, to draw a line between too moist and too dry, because excessively moist conditions, especially soon after planting, will cause the cloves to rot in the ground before sprouting.

Shallots are not subject to any particular problems or any exotic diseases, and their culture is very simple: just keep the plot weeded, drop a bead of fertilizer along the rows about midway in the growing season or whenever there has been a lot of rain, and water well during dry spells. Nothing could require less work than shallots.

Harvest

Shallots tell you when they are ready to pick. The tops turn brown and dry and fall over. When you see that this has happened to most of them, take a rake and knock over the slowpokes. Leave them for a day or two until all have lost their green and at least turned yellow or tan. They are then ready to be gently dug up.

They should dry before being stored, so spread them in a single layer, not touching one another, on plastic or hay or something similar and dry, and leave either in the garage or in an airy shed. They will dry out more quickly if you leave them in the sun for the first few days, but this will mean more work, since you will have to bring them in at night, out of the dew or a possible shower. Once they have cured partially (after a week or so), you may wish to clip off the tops, leaving about an inch of stem above the bulb. For marketing, you might find it interesting to braid the tops, like garlic heads. The braids make very attractive kitchen decorations—like herb wreaths—and can gradually be used up by taking the bottom bulbs when some are wanted for cooking.

Of course you would charge more for the braids than you would for the same amount of shallots simply packed in a tray because you should be compensated for the hand labor involved in making the braids. If you dress up the braids with a bit of ribbon, bought inexpensively in shops that sell the makings for dried-flower arrangements, you will find no one will begrudge you a good price.

Snow Peas (*Pisum sativum macrocarpon*)

Snow peas are not a new vegetable; they have been around a long time. You will find them in early catalogs and garden books under "edible-podded peas," and sometimes they are called sugar peas. In fact most of the varieties have "sugar" in their names, as in Dwarf Gray Sugar and Mammoth Melting Sugar, which should give you some idea of how delicious they are.

For some reason, however, snow peas didn't catch on with the average American gardener until the recently developed interest in Chinese cooking. As almost everyone knows, snow peas are one of the most ubiquitous and popular of Chinese vegetables. What you may not know is that they are incredibly easy to grow and take up very little room in proportion to their yield.

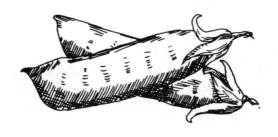

The difference between snow peas and common garden or English peas is that you do not shell the pods to get at the edible portion. The entire pod and its contents are simply picked and eaten—raw if you pick them really young or very briefly cooked, as in stir-fry cooking. Obviously, if you can eat the entire vegetable, you will get a much greater yield than if you only eat the peas and not the pods. The result is that a bowl of snow peas is a bowl of edible vegetable, whereas a bowl of unshelled English peas is a handful of edible vegetable.

Snow peas also require no work. You can pick them a few minutes before you want to cook them, and there is no stringing or shelling or other preparation if they are young. If they are slightly more mature, you may want to string them, but that is very easy. If, on the other hand, they have gotten away from you and have matured, you can still eat them by shelling them like English peas. But they are so delicious that I cannot imagine their staying on the vine so long.

In spite of their ease of growth and high yield, snow peas continue to command exorbitant prices in the produce market. They usually sell for about $4.00 or $5.00 a pound. I cannot think of an easier or more lucrative cash crop.

Appearance

Snow pea vines look almost exactly like English pea vines except that the flowers come in a beautiful lavender (which many seed catalogs describe, for some unknown reason, as reddish) and a clear white. I particularly like the lavender flowers because they remind me of sweet pea flowers, and they are very decorative climbing up the side of my garage in profusion against the pale-green leaves.

If you do not have a place for them to climb (although this is easy to devise), there are dwarf varieties that do not require support and are low-growing and bushy. They are usually named as a dwarf variety, as in Dwarf Gray Sugar, and have the advantage of being earlier than the tall varieties, such as Mammoth Melting Sugar.

A new variety that has been introduced during the last few years is called Sugar Snap. It has apparently swept the gardening world by storm, and garden writers describe it in ecstatic terms. I tried it the second season it was available and, to my surprise, found it vastly inferior to the older varieties. But I am definitely in the minority, so you should try it and see what you think. Do plant it along with one of the standards so that you can compare them dish for dish.

When to Plant

Snow peas prefer cool weather and will quickly burn up in really hot weather. Except for that you could probably grow them right through the spring-to-fall seasons. As it is, you can plant them as early as the ground can be worked. After your initial planting you can plant another lot every ten days until you think they will run into the really hot weather of summer.

A second planting for a fall crop will be very satisfactory. Although the yield will probably not be as great as with your spring planting for the amount of work involved, it will still be well worth your while. And, of course, the demand for them in the market is equally strong all year round.

Where to Plant

Snow peas can be planted anywhere you have full sun. Since they will be finished and removed by at least the end of June, you can use a site that you want later for another vegetable. If you grow a tall variety, plan to site them along a fence or in a place where stretching netting for them to grow on will not shade vegetables growing around or behind them. I grow them in back of a flower and herb garden in front of the house, alongside the garage. I put up brown netting I use to keep birds off my blueberries and raspberries and secure it with just a few brown thumbtacks. When the snow peas are climbing, this is a very satisfactory support. When they are gone, it is invisible against the weathered board and batten side of the garage. Not having to put up supports each season is a great time-saver.

Culture

I find snow pea vines dry out very easily, so I recommend planting the seeds in a trench. That way you can draw up the earth around them as they grow, even ridging it a little as they get tall enough. This protects the lower stems and keeps them green much longer. In addition, give the plants a lot of water; they don't mind wet soil but do mind dryness.

A 10–10–10 fertilizer will give you better results than the standard 5–10–5. Generous applications of manure (especially rabbit or poultry, which is higher in nitrogen), wood ashes, and bonemeal are all good. If you are planning a partially cash crop or want to freeze your surplus, I suggest you dig some of the fertilizer into the bottom of the ditch. Then add a layer of plain soil, into which you plant the seeds. Later on in the growing season lay a bead of fertilizer on both sides of the row and you will have done all the work necessary for a super crop.

Since snow peas should not ever be allowed to really dry out, good mulching practice is essential. It will save you work not only in watering but also in weeding. Once the peas are growing thickly, it is almost impossible to weed them without pulling up some of the vines. A good deep mulch will eliminate both the work and the problem.

If you have poor luck with your snow peas the first time you try them, it may be because your soil is especially deficient in nitrogen. In that case you might want to try a commercial mixture that aids legumes in nitrogen-fixing; this will enable your vines to make the most of the fertilizer. You might find it interesting to dig part of the row with the mixture and part without; the difference in yield might surprise you. If you wish to order it, include it in your seed order, since it should be used when you sow.

Harvest

The only problem with snow peas is keeping them picked. If you do not pick them when they are ready, the vines will think they have completed their job and will stop flowering. This can happen very early in the season and deprive you of most of your crop. When the vines are at their peak you may have to pick twice a day—they are that prolific. But if you can sell them for several dollars a pound, you won't complain about the burden of frequent picking. Let them grow just until the peas become noticeable in the pods. At that point the vegetable will still be delectable, but each pod will be heavier and will be more profitable for the gardener. Sugar Snap peas, which I have mentioned earlier, can be picked when the peas are quite lumpy in the pod and will still be completely edible, but they are the exception.

Do not discard the vines or any unusable pods; they are a rich source of nitrogen and belong on your compost pile or dug into your garden for wintering over. Actually, it is better to dig them directly into your garden; that way all the nitrogen goes into your soil instead of being used to break down the compost. Since nitrogen is the most expensive fertilizer to buy, growing your own—even in this small way—is a saving.

Vegetable Spaghetti

Vegetable spaghetti, also known as spaghetti squash, has become very popular in recent years. It is a variety of winter squash that cooks up into strands of spaghettilike vegetable and is delicious with any of the sauces you would use for real spaghetti. It is also very good cold if mixed with a little oil before cooling. Part of its popularity is due to the fact that it is very low in calories, so people who like spaghetti but want to watch their weight can eat this with a clear conscience.

Although almost unknown a few years ago, spaghetti squash can now be found in almost all produce markets. There is no reason why you could not sell all you can grow, and you may be able to get your crop into the market sooner than the commercial farmers.

Individual squashes usually end up selling for over $1.00 each and it is not unusual for larger ones to run over $2.00. If you charge 59 to 69 cents a pound, their weight will make the per-item price quite high.

Since spaghetti squash is a winter squash, you do not have to sell it unless the price is right. I have kept spaghetti squash through winter and spring without any special care. This gives you a long selling season and a great deal of flexibility in marketing.

Appearance

Spaghetti squash grows to a smooth, large oval, about eight inches long. The young fruits are pale cream, and as they mature they gradually turn a deeper yellow or tan color. The vines are similar in appearance to other squash vines, and the flowers are the familiar large yellow squash blossoms. Since it is a winter squash, it normally requires a large area, but this can be reduced to manageable, small-garden size by training the vines up a fence. If you do this, plan to support the fruits when they become large and too heavy for the vines. Cheesecloth, old nylon panty hose, or any other quick-drying, porous material can be used to make a sling that will hold the fruit securely. An advantage of this system—aside from saving valuable garden space—is that the fruit is kept off the ground and will not rot or be defaced by slugs.

When to Plant

Like all squash, spaghetti squash is frost-sensitive, and the seeds cannot be planted until all danger of frost is past and the ground has warmed up. This is usually around the middle of May or the beginning of June.

Where to Plant

Choose a sunny location in your regular vegetable garden.

How to Plant

Before planting, dig in compost, manure, and fertilizer. Rake the bed smooth and cover with black plastic if you want to warm up the earth more quickly. The black plastic will also serve to prevent weeds from growing while you are waiting to plant your crop.

Seeds should be planted about one inch deep and the earth firmed over them. You may plant either in a hill or in rows. If you plant in a hill, that simply means planting a group of three or four seeds fairly close together, then leaving about 4 feet of space before planting the next hill. It does not mean raising the ground into a hill shape—although if you are doing raised gardening, your bed will, of course, be above the level of the path part of the garden. The germination rate for all squash seeds is fairly high, so it is not necessary to plant twice as many as you mean to end up with and then have the work of thinning out the extra plants. I usually simply plant in rows along the fence, leaving about 18 inches between seeds. This makes for a fairly thick squash patch, but it seems to work out fine. The vines often not only climb the fence but go over it and into the meadow, where it sets its fruit in among the meadow grass. You can avoid this by training the vines to grow along the fence rather than up and over it.

Culture

If you have prepared the soil properly before planting you won't have much work to do the rest of the season. Keep the patch well weeded and well watered. The latter task will be much simpler if you mulch well with compost and salt hay. This will keep the ground moist with a minimum of watering and will also serve to keep the vines and fruit off the damp ground.

The most serious problem you may run into is the squash borer. This unpleasant creature lays eggs on the underside of the squash leaves. When the eggs hatch they turn into fat white "worms," or grubs, that bore into the stems and will quickly destroy the entire vine (at which point they simply move over to the next stem). Dusting the leaves and the ground around the plants with wood ashes sometimes deters the egg laying. If, however, the borer gets into the vine, all is not lost. If you have been keeping an eye on the plant, you will quickly notice the hole where it has gone in and the "shavings" that have collected around the hole. Take a sharp knife and cut from the hole up the vine until you come to the borer. Remove it (an extended paper clip works well) and kill it. You might cut the vine a little farther, because sometimes there are several borers—big ones and little ones. When the inside of the vine looks healthy and untouched, take moist earth and cover the vine from its base to a little above the cut you have made. Keep the earth moist and the vine may soon put out new roots and be as good as new. I sometimes put a little clear plastic over the mounded-up earth so that it won't be washed away in a shower.

The important thing, next to preventing borers entirely, is to catch them when they first get into the vine. Keeping your eye on the garden and watching out for pests is an important part of pest control.

Harvest

You can pick the squash at almost any stage of its growth, but you will naturally not get as big a crop as if you wait until the fruits are matured. Vegetable spaghetti takes about one hundred days to mature, but I usually start picking a couple of weeks sooner because we are very fond of this vegetable and become impatient.

After you have grown it for a season you will get to recognize the look of the mature fruit. It is important to pick it once it has matured or the vine will stop producing new flowers and fruit. It is also important to pick only mature squash if you wish to hold it for any length of time; only mature squash will store well.

To store the squash, wash it well after picking and dry thoroughly. Put in a cool (about 50–55 degrees Fahrenheit) dry, airy place; do not allow the squash to touch one another. It's always a good idea when storing vegetables to look them over once in a while in case one has started to deteriorate. I have had excellent luck storing vegetable spaghetti, and we eat it throughout the winter and spring, so we are deprived of it for only a short season in the summer.

4. Flowers and Other Plants

Originally I thought I would call this chapter "Inedible Cash Crops," but I soon realized that would not do justice to such plants as daylilies, so I have opted for the more general title. As you will see, I have only touched the surface of plants that are commonly grown on landscaped grounds. You will undoubtedly be inspired to make cash crops of many more and may even be influenced in your future landscaping by the market possibilities of one plant over another. Planning with marketing potential in mind will in no way diminish the beauty of your grounds, and it will add interest to the whole gardening process.

Here are some suggestions.

Bittersweet (*Celastrus scandens*)

Bittersweet is a vine that once grew copiously but has been collected so heavily for generations that it has become quite rare even in its native habitat. My mother, who lives in the next village, doesn't have a single vine on her extensive acreage; on the other hand, in recent years I have discovered several vines on my little bit of land. So apparently it will reappear if given half a chance. It's fun in the fall if you live in the country to keep an eye out for it on your woodland walks; it is easy to recognize even before the berries show color and grows high up on any tree or shrub that is nearby.

Bittersweet is sold by almost all florists and garden centers and by many markets, so you can be sure of a market for it as a cash crop. It is easy to collect; all that is needed are a pair of sharp clippers and a plastic bag. If you gather bittersweet before the berries have fully split their yellow outer shells, dropping them in a bag until you get your harvest home will prevent them from being damaged.

If, however, you want to develop really good sources for this crop and get premium prices, you might want to grow the cultivated variety. While the wild will cost you nothing but your time and has a certain sort of Chinese charm of its own, the cultivated variety is much showier. The berries grow in large, thick clusters rather than in the occasional small clusters that occur in the wild, and the effect is really spectacular compared to that of the wild bittersweet.

The only difficulty in growing the cultivated variety—since the cost of a single plant is nominal and you would never need to buy another—is that you may not want to plant bittersweet on your property. In spite of the fact that it has become rare in some areas due to overcollecting, it is a very invasive vine, and I can assure you from personal experience that the first feeling of delight you experience on discovering a vine of wild bittersweet will soon turn to dismay as you spend season after season cutting it off trees, shrubs, walls, and everything else within reach. If I did not keep after it, I am convinced I would soon have a couple of acres of nothing but bittersweet—except for an occasional well-established patch of poison ivy. Of course, if you are growing it as a cash crop, you will probably not have my problem and will be able to keep it under control without any difficulty. Since you will be able to sell all you can grow as soon as your sources find they can depend on you, your crop will never get out of hand.

Bittersweet must be dried before it is sold, but this is no more difficult than clipping the lengths you want and hanging them upside down in a dry, warm place for a week or so. If you just want to sell it in bunches, this is perfectably acceptable. If, however, you take the trouble to make arrangements with it or combine it with other dried material, you will get a higher price for the additional work. A little imagination can pay off handsomely if you have a knack for this sort of thing.

Appearance

Bittersweet, whether wild or cultivated, is a very attractive vine. The foliage is pretty and well shaped. The green fruit turns to yellow in the fall and soon splits open, revealing an inside seed that has been variously described as crimson, orange-scarlet, and red. It is very handsome and lends itself to interesting dried arrangements, especially in baskets and other natural containers. With luck it will last the winter, although toward the end, careless dusting or a bump with the elbow will scatter seeds all over the table and floor. The popularity of bittersweet is dependable, and I think you would find it a very satisfactory addition to your cash crops.

A word of warning is in order concerning the aggressive nature of this handsome vine; it will kill any tree it is allowed to climb undisturbed. The strength of the bittersweet vine is so great that it will actually make grooves in the trunk of any tree it mounts. I think Tarzan could have swung from tree to tree in his jungle quite safely if it had contained bittersweet. If you wish a great harvest, let it climb up dead trees or poles or along fences. Or put it some distance from the nearest tree, so that you have a lot of cuttable material before your little forest is in any danger. If you wish—but I would advise this only with the cultivated variety—you can grow it up a trellis or make a handsome arbor.

When to Plant

Bittersweet is usually planted in the spring and quickly produces a harvestable crop the following fall. At most you might have to wait one more season if the vine is very young.

How to Plant

Bittersweet is totally undemanding; sun or shade makes absolutely no difference to it, and it will thrive in any ordinary garden soil. You may plant nursery stock or propagate plants you already have through root cuttings, layering, or from seed. If you are buying nursery stock, your initial purchase is the only one you will ever make.

Culture

In regard to garden chores, bittersweet may be considered as totally uncultured; it requires absolutely no care on your part to keep it growing and thriving. As I have indicated, your only chore may be keeping it within bounds. Forget about fertilizing, watering, and weeding and just enjoy this splendid vine.

Harvest

Sometime in September you will really notice the green berries that are borne in profusion on the fruiting vines. In no time at all a touch of yellow will appear, and from then on the vines can be cut and hung upside down to dry. Most of the leaves will fall off by themselves in the process (in the cultivated variety you will have few leaves and many berries) and the rest can be removed by hand with just a little care. Since you sell them as soon as they have dried, there is no problem with storage. Just be sure to save some for your own dried arrangements and to give as hostess presents during the fall.

Dahlias

If you have always bought potted dahlia plants and discarded them at the end of the season when the first frost turned them to blackened stumps, you may wonder how they could possibly be a practical cash crop. Actually, their potential is excellent: they are inexpensive to grow, require comparatively little attention, and sell for satisfactorily high prices (satisfactory if you are selling rather than buying).

I discovered this more or less by accident when I found one season that my budget would no longer support the number of dahlias I felt my garden plan required. As an alternative I turned to seeds, which were inexpensive and gave me a much wider choice of varieties. While both roots and plants were out of reach, seeds were no more expensive than those of most other flowers, and I had not tried them sooner only because I have very little room in which to start seedlings in the house.

Since I made the decision to switch to seeds when dahlia plants were already being offered by the local nurseries, I was way past the March deadline for planting them indoors. The chance I took was of not having any flowers until practically frost time. It didn't work out that way; my in-the-ground seeds sprouted fairly promptly—in about twelve days—and flowered so fast they took me by surprise. In no time at all the bed had caught up with my neighbor's bought plants, and it continued to be a mass of blooms until well into fall, when I stopped dead-heading (removing the blossoms before they go to seed).

In the fall, when the plants had been touched with frost, I had a fine crop of roots to sell for the next season. This is a good return for a few pennies, saving money for the home gardener and providing both plants, cut flowers, and roots for cash crops.

Dahlias have been a popular flower since the time of the Aztecs, who called them Acoctli, or water pipe, because of their hollow stems. The native dahlias grew wild around the area that is now Mexico City and were admired by Cortez. King Philip II of Spain took an interest in the flora of the New World and around 1570 sent a Spanish naturalist to study and collect plant material. The naturalist apparently worked at a leisurely pace, since dahlias were not sent to the Royal Gardens at Madrid until 1789.

In spite of this slow start, Europe took dahlias to its collective bosom, and by 1840 enthusiastic professional and amateur gardeners were not only growing dahlias throughout the Continent and Great Britain but were developing many novelties, which commanded excessively high prices. Double dahlias and some of the other varieties we take for granted today originated at this time.

Meanwhile dahlias had come full circle, so to speak, when in 1821 they were brought back to America in their new, cultivated forms. They soon became staples in American gardens, and the American Dahlia Society was formed as proof that this lovely flower now had a firm place in the horticultural landscape. In 1953 the society sponsored a trip to Mexico in order to search for and collect specimens of wild dahlias. The trip was successful, and the collected specimens were brought back to the States and subsequently grown at the New York Botanical Garden. So when you grow dahlias in your garden, you are taking your part in the history of this beautiful plant.

Today there are many classifications of dahlia, from single to miniature to dwarf to pompon and more. Dahlias seem to have the peculiar ability to mimic other flower forms; among the classifications are anemone and cactus. Add to this the enormous range of colors available and the wide variation in heights—from the low-growing miniatures to the more than four-feet-tall giants—and you have a flower that can never be boring.

Try it as a cash crop; it is so versatile that you will not mind giving it space in your garden and will be rewarded, both in beauty and in cash, many times over.

Appearance

It is difficult to describe the dahlia flower because it comes in almost all colors, including blue (which is brand new), single and double-petaled, all sizes, and many shapes. Many of the Dutch varieties are not immediately recognizable as dahlias at all, although a bed of them is a breathtaking sight. The foliage is compact and attractive, and the only possible difficulty is the height of the taller varieties, which require staking. All varieties are suitable for use as cut flowers and are attractive used alone or in combination with other flowers and foliage.

When to Plant

Since I am recommending that you plant seeds, you probably should plant them indoors in March, to be set out around the middle or end of May, when the ground has warmed up. If this is not convenient, start them in the open garden when you can; the plants will be a little late coming to market and you may miss the peak of the selling season, but you will probably still realize a fairly good and steady sale. After the first planting, your own tubers or roots will give you a head start on the season and allow you to get your roots or potted plants out well within the peak period. Seeds will flower the first season they are planted, so you can be sure of a crop of cut flowers no matter which method of propagation you choose.

If you want to gamble on an early spring planting, put black plastic over the bed before you plant; it will warm up much more quickly if you have the usual number of sunny spring days. As soon as you think the treated bed is warm, plant your roots and replace the black plastic. This can start your growing season in April rather than May—a good head start considering you don't have a green-house. If you plant seeds, you can risk setting them out soon after the last frost date in your area; they won't germinate until the soil warms up, but, with luck, they won't rot either and will start growing sooner than you might expect. Since they require 10 to 20 days to germinate, it is important not to delay their start a moment longer than is necessary. Regardless of the variety, dahlias grown from seed will tend to be smaller than those grown from cuttings or roots. This is only true, of course, for the first season, because after that you will have roots.

Where to Plant

Dahlias are very versatile and lend themselves to any number of treatments in the garden. They are very effective in great masses of a single variety and color; on the other hand, a mixed bed of a variety of colors is as gay as flags flying. Because they come in many different heights, they can be used to form a colorful back-ground or a reliable bedding border. And as if all these options were not enough, they can be planted in among other flowers. They are particularly useful because they have a long blooming season—from the time of the first flower until the plant is killed by frost—and do not get that sort of dusty, tatty look that comes to zinnias in the fall.

Most varieties do best in full sun, but there are some, particularly some of the lovely Dutch ones, that will thrive in partial shade.

How to Plant

Dahlias are not fussy about soil as long as the drainage is good; they definitely do not appreciate wet feet. Dig deeply and add plenty of humus and manure to a depth of 12 to 18 inches. If the soil is clayey, add sand to lighten it and plenty of compost to the sand. For your own garden, where results do not have to be so spectacular, this extra preparation is not necessary; for a cash crop, competition requires that your crops be superlative rather than simply good.

If you are planting the giant varieties, set in the stakes when you plant the roots. Place the root with the top end, the one with the live eye, next to the stake, filling in the soil to within a few inches of the surface. Always set the roots in the soil horizontally. Firm the soil and shape it, creating a saucerlike indentation that will hold water. As soon as the root has sprouted and is tall enough, fill in the saucer to normal soil level. If you are setting out plants started indoors, remove the bottom two leaves and plant deep enough to cover the stem just above that point.

If you want to grow from cuttings to increase your yield, take them when the sprouts are at least two inches high. Dip them in hormone rooting powder and set in flats of vermiculite. Be sure to make holes with a pencil or similar tool so that the hormone powder is not brushed off when the stems are set in the holes. Keep the potting mixture moist until the cuttings take hold and start to grow. They can then be potted separately for the market or set out in the ground if it is warm enough.

Dahlia plants will look better if pinched back when they have developed three or four sets of leaves. Remove the top two sets by pinching out. Whether you have to do this or not will depend on the size of the plants you pot for selling. If, however, you take the trouble, your plants will look bushier and more desirable and you can ask a better price. If you are growing the plants for seed or for your own use, you may not want to bother pinching out.

Culture

Dahlias are gross feeders and, for best results, should be fertilized lightly when planted (but do not allow any fertilizer to touch the

roots) and at monthly intervals until the fall. Their only other requirement is copious amounts of water; if the plant stops growing
because of dryness, it will never recover to its full beauty. A 4–12–
4 fertilizer is best, since dahlias like rather more phosphorus than
other flowers.

It is assumed that you are cultivating your flower beds to keep
down the weeds, but dahlias develop feeder roots close to the
surface; after about the first week in September, do not cultivate—
pull up the weeds by hand while they are still in the seedling stage.
This is not much of a chore, because by September weeds are not
growing so profusely and are easier to control.

Harvest

It is clear that the time of harvest depends on the crop. Cuttings
will be available early in the season; cut flowers can be taken
throughout the growing season as soon as the plants start to flower;
individual plants can be potted at almost any time that there is a
demand for them in the market; roots are dug in the fall after the
first frost but usually stored until spring.

You will undoubtedly be storing roots, whether growing dahlias
for your own garden or for sale, and this can be very disappointing
if you find in the spring that none of them have survived the winter.
A few simple precautions will make the difference between success
and failure.

As soon as the frost has blackened the tops, the roots are ready
to be dug. Since they are tender and do not withstand freezing well,
this should be done as promptly as possible.

Use a fork spade to loosen the soil in an area around the roots
before attempting to lift the clump. It is important not to damage
either the root itself or the eye or crown of the plant. If the root is
cut into by the spade, it is vulnerable to disease and rot. As soon
as you have dug up the root, cut the stalk, leaving a two-inch length
attached to the clump.

If the weather is dry and the dew light, leave the roots to dry in
the open sun and air. If the nights are damp, find a covered place
to set them out, not touching one another, for several days. You

might tip the clumps upside down before spreading them out, in case any water has collected in the hollow stalks. The trick in curing the roots is to dry them out sufficiently so that they will not rot, while still leaving them enough moisture to prevent shriveling over the winter. In the beginning you may have a few failures, but experience with your own storage conditions will soon give you a feel for how dry is just right. Some soil will adhere to the clump and should be left there. The excess will fall off as it dries, and the remaining soil will protect the root during storage.

To store the roots, fill a shallow box with two inches of sand, peat moss, or vermiculite. Place the roots on this bed and fill in with more storage material, leaving about an inch of stalk exposed. Store in a cool, but not cold, place; a temperature range of 35–50 degrees Fahrenheit is desirable.

Even the most experienced gardener cannot be sure storage conditions are exactly right, so you should check the roots every so often—at least twice during the winter. If there is any evidence of decay, it should be cut out and the area dusted with dry sulphur. A rotted root should be promptly removed and any roots around it carefully examined at that time and in a few weeks.

If the roots look shriveled, they are too dry and need moisture. The way to treat this condition is to place the shriveled clumps in damp (but not dripping wet) peat moss or moistened sawdust or between layers of wet newspaper. Leave them for a few days, then check to see whether they have recovered. Do not neglect them or they will rot. As soon as they have plumped out and lost the shriveled look, repack as before.

A few weeks before planting time, separate the roots from the clumps with a sharp knife or clippers; do not break them apart with your hands. Sprinkle each root with water and put it on a bed of damp peat moss or sand (this is easy if you simply dampen the bed in which they were stored), then place them in a light, but not sunny, place. Sprinkle them daily with water and watch for the eyes to swell and shoots to appear. Any roots that do not respond to this treatment will not grow and should be discarded.

Plant the roots soon after the shoots appear. If you delay, the roots will get leggy and will not produce the most thrifty plants.

If you are planning to sell the roots, do not do anything except remove them from their winter storage. Examine them carefully so that you do not sell any that have started to shrivel; dissatisfied customers will not buy from you again.

Special Marketing Note:

If you are selling roots, a problem may arise with the way they are kept in the market. It is best to offer them in small carton lots, packed in the same kind of material in which they are stored over the winter, with a label clearly identifying the variety and color the root will produce. This will help ensure that they will not dry out while waiting to be sold; customers are quite accustomed to digging down to find the roots they want.

Another common way of packaging them is individually in labeled plastic bags. Look in the stores to see how other growers have solved the marketing problem and choose the one that is easiest and least expensive for you.

Daylilies

Daylilies grow freely along the roadside and wherever else they have established a territory. This can be in the most unexpected places. There is one area along the New Haven Railroad where daylilies have formed a mass along an eighth of a mile of track. When the clump is in bloom it is breathtakingly lovely. In spite of their free habit of growth in America, daylilies are not natives but were brought to this country from the Far East, and have escaped to become one of our most prolific wild flowers.

As a cash crop daylilies have many things to recommend them: they are trouble-free, prolific, popular, and easy to grow. A small clump, potted, sells for a surprisingly high price, and hybrid species are especially in demand. These are not a crop for the florist—although I have seen many people on the train with bunches of daylilies they are bringing back to the city—but for the local nursery or to sell direct to the consumer. The roots are easy to dig and pot,

and once you have an established clump, the supply will go on forever.

The name "daylily" arises from the fact that each flower lasts only a day. This may be hard to believe if you look at a clump that is a mass of flowers for several weeks, but careful observation will reveal that it is so.

If you wish to start inexpensively, you can gather daylilies from clumps of wild flowers; a small clump will soon grow out-of-bounds. For a cash crop, it is a better way to order selectively from your seedsman. Almost all catalogs contain some daylilies, but for the more unusual varieties, look for catalogs that more or less specialize. Many bulb catalogs will include daylilies, and they will have hybrids that are not generally offered in more general catalogs. The more unusual the varieties you grow, the more you can ask for your crop and the greater the chance that you will get a reputation among local gardeners for having interesting stock.

Lemon lilies—sometimes known as custard lilies—are an exception to the rule that the unusual is what you should aim at; they are universally loved, and many gardeners prefer to grow them to the exclusion of all other lilies. Your biggest problem will be choosing among all the varieties that are available. I would suggest that you collect the wild daylilies if you wish an orange flower. If you are ordering from a seedsman, I think you will do better with yellow, pink, or red flowers; they will be less likely to be confused with the wild lilies and will be more interesting, both in your garden and to your customers.

Appearance

Daylilies have large trumpet-shaped flowers that come in bright, clear shades of orange, yellow, pink, and an odd shade of red (not at all like a rose-red). So far, efforts to produce a blue flower have not met with success. The variations in color are considerable, and a very interesting garden could be designed with only daylilies in it.

The foliage is medium green and flat-bladed, like iris but more delicate and not upright in habit. The flowers rise on tall stalks out of the leafy clumps. Most daylilies are about 3 feet in height, although certain varieties grow to 8 feet and dwarf lilies are available that grow to only 2 feet.

When to Plant

Since you are not planting seed or seedlings, daylilies can be set out anytime that the roots are available. If you are gathering wild plants, suit your own convenience. If you are ordering from the seedsman, note that spring delivery is the usual time. If you are dividing your own clumps, do it in early spring or in the fall so that you will not lose the season's bloom and will give the new clump time to get acclimated.

Where to Plant

Daylilies are lovely everywhere. Unless you have the dwarf variety, they should be planted in back of the flower bed so that they will not shade the shorter flowers. If you have a bank near the road or an area on the grounds that lends itself to naturalizing, take advantage of daylilies to create a large area of these bright flowers. With wild daylilies, be careful where you put them, because they will spread rapidly and be difficult to root out. This makes them very useful for some problem areas but could cause trouble in a peony or rose bed.

How to Plant

Nothing could be simpler. Dig up the roots, or order them from your seedsman, and plant just below the surface of well-worked soil that has been fertilized and combined with well-rotted manure. Water occasionally until roots have had time to establish themselves and then treat with benign neglect.

Culture

Nothing could require less care than daylilies; they don't even need full sun and will do equally well in shade. Watering is no problem since they are equally happy with dry or moist soil, and they never seem to require fertilization, although it is necessary if you wish to keep the clumps blooming at the center. Because daylilies are heavy feeders, they will deplete the soil eventually and the center of the clumps will be all foliage but no flowers. The spreading circumference of the clump will continue to bloom in any case, so you don't have to fertilize if you don't want to, but blooms in the middle will gradually die out.

As I mentioned before, each flower blooms for only one day, but it is not necessary to remove the faded blooms.

Harvest

If you are gathering roots to pot for selling, the best time is in the early spring or fall; it will depend on when your potential customers are looking for this kind of plant material. There is no problem, because the lilies will always be there waiting; you can try out a few pots, see how they go, and be guided accordingly. In my experience, most people plan their gardens and plantings in the spring, and the bulk of your sales will come during that period. You can, however, stimulate out-of-season sales by pointing out solutions to common problems. For instance, when perennial beds run into problems—such as a stand of lupines dying out or delphiniums doing poorly—suggest that daylilies would provide a trouble-free replacement of about the same height. A gardener who has had really bad luck with delphiniums may fall in with your suggestion for a trouble-free bloom very readily.

If you have planned your varieties wisely, you will have lilies blooming from early to late summer, and it might be worthwhile to point this out to prospective purchasers so that they will end up buying several varieties instead of just one. This is an easy way to increase unit sales, and your customers will be delighted with the results.

There is one other crop from daylilies that can be very lucrative. The buds can be dried and sold to specialty shops and Chinese markets as "golden needles." Golden needles are very highly thought of in Chinese cuisine and keep for a long time if carefully dried and stored the same way you store any dried product. Tiger lilies are the variety most commonly used for golden needles, and they can be harvested throughout the blooming season, because the daylong blooms provide a continuous crop of buds. You will be amazed at how much you can charge for golden needles once your sources gain confidence in your product. In the beginning you might wish to give a sample to the store so that they can use it themselves and be convinced that you have produced the genuine (and delectable)' product.

Packaging golden needles is no problem; simply use plastic bags or small, inexpensive clear-plastic containers. The advantage in using the containers is that they are easier to label and can be more neatly stored or shelved, but many Chinese stores are used to the plastic bags and may prefer them. In that case be sure to put on the label before you fill the bag.

Johnny-jump-ups (*Viola*)

I imagine that almost everyone is familiar with Johnny-jump-ups, but in case you do not know this charming old-fashioned flower, it is a tiny, pansy-faced biennial that blooms in the spring. The ancestor of garden pansies, Johnny-jump-ups are still an early spring standby for bedding and rock garden areas and a favorite with children.

A quick look through my collection of garden catalogs failed to turn up any plant or seed offerings; I have always bought them locally along with pansies and other early spring flowers. They are usually sold in small boxes of six or twelve plants. It is very easy to grow them from seed, but, since they are biennials, they will not bloom until the following season. For this reason I suggest that in this impatient world it is easier to buy a few plants. You will never have to buy any again, and they are among the most inexpensive of garden materials.

Although Johnny-jump-ups do not fit the criteria of crops chosen for this book, in that they do not sell for large sums, I am personally very fond of them and feel that their 5-and-10-cent qualities—volume rather than an initial high profit—make them worthy of inclusion here. Whether you choose to grow them for profit depends on how you value your time; growing them is no trouble, since they take care of that aspect themselves, but putting them in boxes and getting them to market may not yield enough cash for you to feel it is worthwhile. On the other hand, whereas a customer will buy a few pots of lilies or a single flat of pachysandra, she or he will often buy a dozen boxes of Johnny-jump-ups. Gardeners like them for bedding and for rock gardens. They are also good tucked in among other flowers to fill out a border or a bare spot.

If you want to take the trouble, you can sell them for a fairly high price by combining them with other small plants in basket or dish gardens. The plants are small and respond well to cutting back. They are easy to keep in the house because they will bloom in less than full sun, and they combine well with other small plant material. An attractive small basket filled with Johnny-jump-ups, violets, a bit of delicate ivy, and a ferny bit of foliage would be a welcome hostess gift, especially if a little tag indicated that all the plants could be set out in the garden when no longer wanted in the house.

Johnny-jump-ups also make pretty nosegays for small containers, such as those you might offer your guests at a dinner party as tiny take-home flower favors.

The nice thing about Johnny-jump-ups as a cash crop is that they will cost you nothing to grow, so your profit depends entirely on your marketing skill.

Appearance

As I have already indicated, Johnny-jump-ups look like miniature pansies; since they are first cousins, this is no surprise. If you wish, they can be grown to form a large mass in the garden area, but after the first year or so you may have to transplant seedlings each spring to achieve the effect you want, because the plants will pop up all over the place and thin out where they grew originally.

When to Plant

Johnny-jump-up boxes are usually sold in early spring along with the first pansies. They can be set in the ground right away. If you prefer to grow from seed—and can find some—they can be planted in early spring, during the summer, or even in the fall. In addition, you can propagate from the roots or from cuttings at almost any time.

Where to Plant

The choice of a site depends on what you want the plants for—for the rock garden or as a bedding plant. The site usually suggests itself as you make your garden plan. For a cash crop it doesn't really matter, because that means you plan to grow Johnny-jump-ups from now on, and the choice of site will depend on where they self-sow; your job will be not to mistake them for weeds and pull them up. They will appear, almost spontaneously, all through the bed in which you first plant them and will spill over onto the lawn. It's a little bit like picking up pennies: you may just leave some if they are too hard to get at.

As with most violas (pansies, for instance), Johnny-jump-ups like but do not require sun. If you have to choose between a dry sunny spot and a semishady moist one, go for moisture every time. The soil should be rich and humusy, full of compost and leaf mold, with added well-rotted manure. Regular light mulching will keep the soil rich in organic matter and give you an abundant crop. It will also cut down on the chore of watering during dry spells.

Because they self-sow so readily, I would suggest you think twice about planting Johnny-jump-ups on a slope. If you do, the original planting will quickly move downhill, and the bed will end up empty on top and crowded on the bottom. Since you will probably be transplanting in any case, this may not matter, but if the slope ends in lawn, you will be digging most of your stock out of the lawn after a very few seasons.

Culture

Properly preparing the soil, watering it so that it never dries out completely, and mulching lightly are the entire cultural requirements of Johnny-jump-ups. I have never noticed any disease or other problems.

The plants bloom profusely and will keep on blooming well into the summer if you dead-head. After a while you will notice that the plants are getting taller and somewhat spindly. At this point you can simply shear them back, flowers and leaves both, to a more attractive height. After a short rest period the plants will put out new leaves and more flowers. At some point a little benign neglect will allow them to mature and self-sow, so that you have an effortless crop, multiplied many times over, the next season.

Harvest

The flowers may be picked at any time. You may dig the plants as needed, always leaving enough to furnish propagation stock for the next year. Study the local market to find out the best time to sell your crop. You may be able to beat the season by a week or so or you may be able to supply the stores with Johnny-jump-ups when commercial nurserymen are no longer bothering. Always take advantage of the fact that your venture is small and therefore more flexible. You do not have to plan as far ahead and you do not have to have as wide a margin of profit as commercial growers, so you can make the most of whatever you have to sell in terms of changing market conditions. Be imaginative; sometimes commercial growers get in a rut—like department stores that show hot, woolly fall clothes in the middle of the summer when what you really want is a new bathing suit.

Lily of the Valley (*Convallaria majalis*)

In flower markets, potted lily of the valley pips sell from $2.50 up for two pips—at least in my area. When I think what a nuisance this lovely flower can be if its spread is not controlled, I am astonished that there is still a commercial market for the pips. There obviously is, however, so you might as well profit by it.

Lily of the valley is not only the traditional bridal flower, it is also an excellent ground cover, and does well in shady places where little else will grow. It should generally be omitted from the perennial flower bed, since it is so difficult to keep within bounds; a bed of just lily of the valley is manageable, especially if the escapees can be mowed down with the rest of the lawn.

Flower shops and markets like to sell pots of pips in the spring, and the prices these plants bring are so high, considering how easy it is to grow them, that it is almost impossible not to make a good profit—even including the cost and time involved in potting.

Since the pink-lilac variety is not often found, you should be able to ask a premium price for pots of this variety. You might even suggest to flower shops that bunches of these might be nice for a wedding at which the bridesmaids wear pink dresses; the bride would carry the usual white variety.

If you like to use lily of the valley as a cut flower, you should be aware that the water in which the flowers stand should be disposed of immediately upon removing the flowers and leaves. Do not use either flowers or leaves to decorate salads or any other foods since lily of the valley is poisonous when ingested. Occasionally I have seen the food column of a newspaper suggest the flowers as decorative additions to salads; I often wonder how many readers became ill after following this unfortunate suggestion.

Appearance

The leaves, flowers, and scent are attractive and often used for brides' bouquets. The oval, slightly cupped leaves grow individually and are as long as the stemmed flower, so it is very easy to shape a bouquet or a flower arrangement composed entirely of lily of the valley. The scent is delicate but pervasive and will be noticeable even in a mixed bouquet. The flowers are bell-shaped and appear in a cluster at the top of the stem. They are traditionally white, but a pink variety—actually pink-lilac—can sometimes be found. Lily of the valley is a welcome addition to almost any property, and you will find it no hardship to include it for both its beauty and its money-making potential.

When to Plant

Early spring, when the pips have just started to show themselves, or late fall, long after blooming, are the best times to plant or move lily of the valley. If after a few years the bed has become overcrowded (fewer or smaller blooms will signal this condition), the bed should gradually be dug up and thinned out. You can then either plant the surplus elsewhere on your grounds or offer them for sale.

How to Plant

The pips should be set in a hole big enough to allow the roots to be arranged unbroken, with an inch of soil above the pip. If you are moving mature plants, plant the little nob at the root of the leaves an inch below the soil surface and firm the soil so that the plant stands upright. It is not necessary to plant closely since the pips will spread rapidly, and the bed will benefit by a light mulch in the beginning. Nine plants to a square yard is the rule of thumb.

Culture

Lily of the valley will grow in almost any soil, but best results will be obtained by the addition of peat moss and leaf mold or compost. The site should be shaded or partly shaded—this is not a sun-loving flower—and well drained.

Since the plants require a season of frost in order to bloom the following season, be sure that any dug but not sold in the fall are placed in sphagnum moss or some similar material for a month or two of cold weather. If dug after frost, they should be thawed gradually before being brought to a warmer temperature.

Harvest

After the pips are dug from their cold storage they can be brought indoors to a temperature no higher than 60 degrees Fahrenheit. Pot them in damp sand or sphagnum moss and keep the growing medium moist. This will keep the plants growing slowly. If you want to speed up growth, depending on your market's requirements, put the pots in a warmer room as soon as the pips peep above the surface of the soil. This will force them into bloom more quickly, but, like all forced plants, the blossoms will not be as long-lasting. It is probably a good idea to have some of each so that you can fill any orders you may get. Sometimes early pots of flowering plants command a much higher price. It will take about a month for the pips to go from potting to blossoms.

Pachysandra (*Pachysandra terminalis*)

One of the most popular and reliable ground covers, pachysandra is found in old garden books under the name Japanese spurge, but that is seldom used today. There is a steady market for it, yet you can crop it every year—and even oftener if you like—without ever making a dent in your own planting. It usually sells in flats of 25, 50, or 100 plants, at $6.50 or more for the largest flat. Since it is easy to fill flats of it in no time at all, you could realize a good steady business selling just pachysandra to landscapers who do large estates as well as to small nurseries and markets.

The chances are you already have some pachysandra growing on your property. If not, discover its virtues for your own grounds and reap the benefits as a cash crop forever after.

Appearance

Pachysandra plants form a dense green carpet of evergreen leaves, about six inches high, which is decorative and a welcome sight throughout the year, even in cold climates. It never gets tacky-looking, never needs cutting back, and it isn't even necessary to cut off the flowers.

For a striking effect, interplant with early spring bulbs, such as grape hyacinth or scilla. The bulbs will bloom on schedule, and then the foliage will die down, leaving the green carpet of pachysandra an unbroken vista for the rest of the year.

When to Plant

Pachysandra can be planted anytime during the growing season, but there will be much less work if you choose either spring or fall. The heat and dryness of summer will make it necessary to water, and perhaps mulch, much oftener to get the bed established, and the leaves of the newly set plants are liable to get a slightly rusty, sunburned look. An early spring planting will get off to a better start with minimum care, and a fall planting will ensure a well-established bed by spring.

Where to Plant

Pachysandra's only requirement is shade; it does not do well in full sun, although it will tolerate a partly sunny location. Pick a spot where almost nothing else will grow because it is too shady and you will have ideal conditions for pachysandra. This means you can plant it under a tree for a neat circle of greenery around the trunk or mass it along a stone wall or as a foundation planting on the shady side of the house.

It is not advisable to plant it in a flower bed unless it is severely restricted by metal or plastic stripping set into the bed so that its top edge is at ground level; if this is not done, your flower bed will soon turn into a pachysandra bed, and everything else will be crowded out. It is one of the few plants I know of that will conquer lily of the valley plantings.

How to Plant

As I have said, pick a spot where almost nothing else will grow because it is too shady and you will have near perfect conditions.

If you have bought a flat of plants, simply separate the individual plants, cutting apart the roots if necessary, and set them in the prepared soil. Water well and mulch with peat moss, digging it in to mix a little with the soil so it doesn't form an impenetrable surface crust. How close you set the plants is a matter of personal choice; it is true that ground covers will eventually fill up any space between plants, but you may not like the look of the site in the meanwhile. I prefer to set them fairly close together and add more to any spots that do not fill in quickly enough.

Pachysandra will spread quickly once it takes hold, but people are often disappointed that their pachysandra has not taken over after the first season. You may find it easier to accept if you remember the old saying: "The first year it sleeps. The second year it creeps. The third year it leaps." I have found this literally true. If the high initial cost of setting out pachysandra means that a large area will go bare for a couple of years, mulch it with pine-bark chips—which you can later rake up to put somewhere else or incorporate in the soil as organic matter—and the area will look neat while waiting. On the other hand, you can skip the purchase of plants and ask for cuttings from friends and neighbors. If they know anything about their garden, they will freely give you all you want; it won't disturb their plantings and will be little work to provide you with hundreds of cuttings.

Although you can plant it in any soil with practically no preparation, pachysandra will respond to a little special care. For a cash crop it is worth doing it by the book. Dig up the prosposed site to a depth of 6 to 8 inches and mix in a lot of peat moss, some well-rotted manure, and a little fertilizer. Ordinarily, since you are interested in leafy top growth, you would expect to use a high-nitrogen fertilizer, but since this is comparatively expensive, the usual 5–10–5 will do fine; pachysandra just isn't that demanding. It does, however, require acid soil, so use an acid fertilizer, such as that you use for your azaleas and rhododendrons; it will not do well in an alkaline soil.

If you are planting under a tree, you may not be able to dig as deeply as suggested without disturbing tree roots (depending on the kind of tree). In that case it is all right to prepare a shallower bed, but dig in a little more peat moss and fertilizer a couple of times a season until the ground is completely covered with plants. From then on, an occasional application of fertilizer, simply broadcast in among the plants, is more than enough attention. Do not try to grow pachysandra under lilacs, because lilacs are alkaline-loving plants and will not enjoy the acid fertilizer; also lilacs are heavy feeders and will resent any plants that eat from the same table they do.

To increase your crop from your own planting—either for your use or to sell—take either cuttings or roots or plants with roots attached. To root cuttings, cut off the top of the plant, taking a cutting with several top leaves but leaving enough stem and leaf for the remaining plant. Dip the stem ends in a root-promoting mixture, such as Rootone, and set in a hole in a soil mixture of two-thirds peat moss and one-third perlite or vermiculite. Be sure you have made the hole with a stick or pencil so that you do not brush off the rooting powder while inserting the stem in the potting mixture. Firm the soil around the stem, and when you have filled the flat with cuttings, water well. The peat moss, of course, should be thoroughly moist before being mixed with the vermiculite. This can be done directly into flats for selling; as soon as the cuttings have started to root and show signs of growth, the flats are ready for market.

Taking cuttings will not disturb an established bed; if anything, it will stimulate growth. Incidentally, if you have room for the bed to spread, an easy way to speed up the process is to rake the border of the planting gently, being careful not to disturb young plants that have already spread into that area. Then fertilize lightly and mulch thinly with peat moss. Weed, if necessary, but do not worry about digging up grass—just clip it back a little. Water occasionally, and in no time at all your border will be thick with plants and making a further foray into the area by the next season. I have tripled the size of a bed on a hill below my driveway by this simple method and with practically no work at all.

On the other hand, if the plants are spreading in areas you wish to keep lawn, either mow the border you wish to maintain (which will discourage the pachysandra and encourage the grass) or set in a metal or plastic rim border just up to soil level, taking care that it is not any higher or it will interfere with the lawn mower. These retaining rims come in round packages and are carried by most hardware stores and garden centers.

Another way to propagate pachysandra is by roots. This requires a very decisive approach, because one root leads to another, and you have to be firm about taking only what you need. Simply grasp a plant firmly and pull. If your soil is the way it should be, the plant will come up easily, trailing a long white root (or several) with tiny, hairlike roots growing from it. Chances are that if you continue pulling you will soon find yourself with numerous plants and miles of roots. Since this would be unmanageable and might lead to an unsightly bed, do not pull up too much. Lift the roots and two or three plants, cut the end roots off with shears or clippers, then separate the mass into individual plants (this will mean more clipping). With care you can get one plant and one root. The root will probably be longer than you can plant easily, but simply bend it and wind it around itself, tucking the end into the wrapped-around root. This will give you a nice compact bundle of roots, with the plant stem upright and a twined root that can be set neatly in a hole. With this system it is easy to plant a neat bed, setting out the roots and cuttings at regular intervals. If you attempt to plant the long root without tying it up in a neat package, you will soon have a bed of interplanted roots, and in no time at all you will be digging up what you have planted in trying to plant more.

Since it is most efficient to complete one stage before moving on to the next, plan to collect all your roots or cuttings before you plant any. They will keep for a long time in a pail of water, and a pail will hold a large number of plants. Set the pail in a shady spot until you are ready to plant. The plants can stay this way safely for a while, but after a time they will begin to grow in the water. If this happens, you will have a messy tangle of roots and will only make unnecessary work for yourself. So try not to let the pail go untended more than a week.

You can plant these roots directly into flats or in an in-ground bed, depending on whether they are for your own use or for sale. If they are for sale, check locally to find the number of roots usually sold in a flat and put an equal number, or a few more, in your flats.

Pachysandra flats can be filled either with individual plants complete with roots or with stem cuttings clipped from the top few inches of your bed. Since pachysandra spreads wherever it is allowed to, and since it forms suitable stem cuttings steadily, you will never run out of plant material. Both kinds of flats should be prepared about a month before you plan to sell them; the stem cuttings may take longer but can be speeded up if you first dip the stem in rooting hormone powder, then stick into holes made with a pencil, fertilize with acid fertilizer, and keep moderately moist.

With your buckets full of pachysandra, you can then take your time and plant the flats at your leisure. The flats should be filled with a mixture of vermiculite, potting soil, and peat moss and kept damp. To plant, make a hole with a pencil. Take a plant, shorten the root if necessary, and wind it around itself. Then insert it into the hole and tamp down the earth firmly around it. Make all the holes before you start to work or you will not fit in the correct number. Winding the root around itself creates a compact plant; if you pull the end of the root through one of the loops you have thus made, you will create a little loose sort of knot that will hold together nicely. It will not fit into as small a hole as will stem cuttings, but you can still get one hundred in a standard flat easily, and crowding doesn't hurt pachysandra.

Harvest

Since there is no fruit or even any flowers worth cutting, the only crop is more pachysandra, which we have covered under culture. There is truly no limit to what can be done by way of increasing a crop of pachysandra cuttings or roots. From an original flat of fifty plants bought at a church fair I now have two large areas completely covered and my mother now has all she can use on her grounds. I have also filled a large area under a neighbor's dogwood trees and have donated flat after flat to charity sales. The only reason I am not innundated with pachysandra is that I have given firm instructions to keep it within bounds by merciless mowing.

Pachysandra does not seem to be subject to pests and diseases. Occasionally a patch will seem to run into a problem that shows up in the leaves in early spring. I ignore it, and by summer the patch is back to normal.

Crops into Cash

5. How to Market Your Vegetable Crops

The way to realize cash from your crops is to sell them, and this means you have to learn something about marketing. If you have only a few extra tomatoes or a couple of pounds of green beans, you will not need to do anything more than take them to your local market and ask the produce department manager if he would like to buy them from you. This will bring in some change, but I hope you have something more ambitious in mind. Without going into full-scale market gardening, it is possible to make an impressive amount on the surplus from even a small garden. Since I imagine most of my readers already have a garden—although there is nothing to prevent the new gardener from taking advantage of the advice in this book—the difference between growing plants and vegetables for one's own enjoyment and growing a cash crop will be a matter of degree and of planning. The first year will only show you the possibilities, because you will be learning a new skill. Also, some of the information you need to gather is seasonal, and it will take observation over the year as this data becomes available.

Think of it as a business, even if only on a small scale, and it will be much more successful and more fun.

Do Your Own Marketing Study

Since you will be selling locally, your first job is to study your local market. Fortunately, since you will probably limit yourself to your own town and perhaps the city nearest you, direct observation is the simplest and cheapest method. Where a large company would have to hire a market research firm and gather all sorts of statistics, you can simply go window-shopping. What you want to know is which items will sell best that fall into the category of what you want to grow (or may already be growing).

First make some lists. In making your lists, eliminate items you would never include in your own garden, such as pineapples, sweet potatoes, peanuts, and similar crops. Even though many of them can be grown in most parts of the country, with a little special care in the colder areas, they are not worth the trouble and will generally not produce plentifully. (I got a big kick out of growing sweet potatoes and peanuts in Connecticut, but I would never choose them for cash crops.)

Make a list of everything that grows on your property: vegetables, flowers, small shrubs, ground covers, and other small plant material. Now go out to the markets with pad and pencil and see what is selling for a dollar or more a pound. This is where the seasonal part of your observation comes in—because, obviously, eggplant will be cheaper when it is ripening in local gardens than in the middle of a frosty winter when it is coming in from Florida or Mexico or other distant places. All vegetables have a season, with seasonal variation in prices; the more an item is in season, the lower the price. You may have been aware of this in a general way, but now you want to know exactly how the seasons rise and fall. Your local extension office will send you a chart showing the growing season for various vegetables and plants in your area, but you should do your own research on prices because this is an important part of your marketing plan. Clearly, you won't have much choice the first year; you will have to sell whenever the surplus produce is available in your garden. After the first year, planning will enable you to take advantage of the higher prices commanded by out-of-season produce. This doesn't mean you have to have a greenhouse; beating the season by even a week or two can make a big difference in your profits.

Keep two lists according to markets: one to study the market, one recording your own sales. For the market-study chart, make the list of crops along the right-hand side of the page. (See the May Market-Study Chart below.) Then make a column for each market. Since there probably won't be more than three or four, the columns can be fairly wide. This will enable you to divide them into two columns: one to check when that market has that item and one in which to write the price. If you make your form and then make copies of it, you will be able to do a different form for different times of the year: for example, January, March, May, June, etc., depending on the different times the produce you are interested in comes into the market in your area. If you really like this part of your planning, you could even do a market-study chart of the particular items you plan to sell and could then see at a glance when the peak prices occur. The difference between the price of early raspberries and in-season raspberries is breathtaking; raspberries, however, are not really a good example, because even at the peak of season they are so expensive. (The moral being that you should be sure to put raspberries on your list if at all possible.)

When you're ready to make a chart of your sales, your account book will give all the information you need: item sold, date sold, price paid you, and retail price at which the store sold your item (this will tell you the store's markup). In addition, your account book will show how large an order was sold and enable you eventually to weed out markets placing too small orders.

In studying prices for the purposes of the chart, use the retail price. It will be a more accurate guide to what the item will sell for to the consumer—that is, how much of a premium the consumer is willing to pay for out-of-season produce. The produce manager may not give you the full benefit of this inflated price, but it is still the season you should aim at.

May Market-Study Chart		
Village Market	Organic Market	Crop
$1.25 lb.	$2.25 lb.	Jerusalem artichokes
.49 bunch	.45 bunch	scallions
3.99 lb.	4.25 lb.	snow peas
_____	_____	pachysandra

Note: Always include all the crops you could sell that month even though, as in the above example of pachysandra, those markets may not carry that particular crop.

One of the reasons for making this list has to do not with pricing but with the nature of your local market. There are local variations in taste, and certain items sell better in one part of the country than in others. Eggs, for instance, come white and brown, and although there is no difference nutritionally, in certain areas there is a marked preference for brown eggs. The hens neither know nor care whether they lay brown or white eggs, and either way the cost is the same to the farmer, but in areas where brown eggs are preferred, they cost more money—for no good reason except that the consumer will pay more for them. I am not suggesting that you take to raising chickens, I am just pointing out that if you did, in this instance you could make a lot more money by raising chickens that laid brown eggs rather than white.

If you want to grow something you can't find in any of the markets, do not automatically assume there is no market for it and you had therefore better forget about it. Not so long ago no market carried vegetable spaghetti and no one knew how to cook it. I grew it and gave it to my friends and neighbors, who loved it. Suddenly one day it started appearing in the local markets, and many gardeners included it in their vegetable gardens. Now it is everywhere, and recipes for it are found in all the newspapers and magazines. This can happen with something you introduce if your market is willing to take a chance on it and you help it along with recipes or a note about what it is and how to use it. What you have to decide during your window-shopping expedition is whether the consumers in your area are adventurous and will try something new. The range of items in the markets you look at will give you a clue. Avocados, bean sprouts, alfalfa sprouts, vegetable spaghetti, shallots, and similar items will hint at cooks that will welcome new items and will at least try them out.

If you are pinning your plans mostly on scallions and asparagus, you won't need to worry; these have a ready market everywhere. But if you want to grow asparagus peas, you need to know the nature of your buying public. In the beginning it would be wise to stick to sure things; if you label your produce, you will create a public that knows your products and will trust you when you introduce a new item.

Now that you've done your market survey, the next step is to set up your production plan. This calls for a list of what you are already growing. You probably have this from the garden plan you make at the beginning of the season, so pull it out and compare it, item by item, with the market lists you've just made. Once you have done this, you will be able to see at a glance where you are missing out on profitable items. For instance, I feel that raspberries should be number one of any cash crop, wherever there is room for a raspberry bed. You will quickly see from your list that raspberries are very profitable and are sure bets. After all, they are no harder to grow than tomatoes or zucchini—in fact, in many ways they are easier—but bring in a much greater return. Also, with proper selection of varieties, raspberries can yield a crop both early and late. The characteristics that makes raspberries an unsatisfactory commercial crop—their delicacy and poor shipping qualities—are not problems for the local gardener, and the price has already been set so high that, even if you charge somewhat less at first, you will realize a great deal of money from a single season.

On the other hand, you will see that zucchini will never be worth the space and trouble in terms of its return. While it is probably a vegetable you will always grow for your own table, it is not a crop I would recommend as a cash crop for small-scale growing.

Weed Out Your Vegetables

Planning for cash crops is a little different from planning for your own use. Now you have to consider not only what your family likes to eat but also whether or not you are using your gardening space efficiently.

Take your garden-plan list and look at it from this point of view. I am assuming that you have a limited amount of space, or at least a limited amount of time you can spend on the garden, so you cannot really afford to increase the garden area appreciably. This means possibly displacing or replacing some of the crops you usually grow. For example, if you grow onions, you may want to give up some or all of their space to shallots and garlic. This does not mean that you will have to give up cooking with onions—a step I could never contemplate—but it means that you will buy onions instead of growing them. I know that at first this will be a wrench; I find my onions ever so much better and sweeter than the ones in the market. If you are going to be businesslike, however, you will soon recognize that growing area as too valuable to be turning out onions when it can be producing shallots. The money you will make from the sale of the shallots will pay for the onions, with a nice profit left over. Of course, if you still want to grow some onions, you can always divide the area, using just a portion for shallots.

Go over everything you grow with this kind of perspective. If you have been growing green beans and can buy them just as fresh from a local farmer, maybe that space could be put to better use as an asparagus bed or for hot peppers. I must admit that the thought of not growing my own beans bothers me, and I would not consider eliminating them unless I was sure of a good source of equally good garden beans. I worry each season that local corn will no longer be available and I will have to go back to growing my own.

Another way of increasing the efficiency of your garden is to plan more carefully the size of the area devoted to a particular crop. It may be that you are in a bit of a rut and are growing more than you can really use. Or it may be that your garden plan is the same as it was a few years ago when you had the time to can or freeze the surplus. Now you may have a part- or full-time job and are not really making the most of your surplus. If you have to look for friends to take your extra vegetables, and if these are not vegetables on the list of ones that are good for a cash crop, you are growing too many. Do not be sentimental in weeding out surplus vegetables; even tomatoes may be more abundant than they need be.

Efficient Gardening

Gardening for pleasure often leads to certain habits that are not efficient. When you are growing cash crops, even if only as an adjunct to your usual gardening, the challenge is to make them as profitable as possible. This means cleaning up your gardening habits. All the usual chores—spring tilling, fertilizing, watering—can be done without a real plan, or they can be done systematically, as a farmer does them. Any cut in expenses and any saving along the way assume especial importance because they add to the profit side of the ledger. For instance, you may never have bothered with a compost heap. With the price of fertilizer rising each season, and sure to continue to do so, the efficient gardener has to think of a compost heap. Perhaps you might decide to plow the first season's profits into building a bin for compost or getting one of the commercial composters. You might be a little freer about ordering a good supply of horse manure to rot nicely (and without odor) in a corner of your backyard.

You might find that purchasing the various fertilizers and mixing them yourself works out more cheaply than buying the mixes (5–10–5, etc.). If this should be the case, not only would you save money but you would also be able to fertilize more selectively, because you could mix a high-nitrogen fertilizer for those vegetables that need it and a more general combination for those that do not. A variation on this is to buy a separate supply of nitrogen fertilizer and add it to a standard mix when needed. Remember that there are many sources of nitrogen in material you may think of as waste, such as corn fodder, cow manure, eggshells, fish wastes (including shellfish), salt hay, tea grounds, and other substances. (See the source list below.) If you add these to your compost heap, you may create a high-nitrogen fertilizer at no cost at all. Legumes are naturally nitrogen-fixing, and growing them in a plot the season before you plant a crop that requires high nitrogen will give you a naturally nitrogen-rich soil the following year.

Once you think of your garden as a supply of cash as well as food, you may find yourself taking an interest in good management and wanting to learn more about the technical side of gardening. Of course, if you already have a green thumb and enjoy great crops, just keep on the way you are with a few adjustments in crop selection as suggested throughout the book.

Whatever you do, don't fight nature. Every gardener finds some crops do better than others in his/her garden. Sometimes even two neighbors, side by side, will find differences in how their gardens produce: one will do well with eggplant but not melons, while the other will produce prize-winning melons but have no luck at all with eggplant. If you have had one or two poor seasons with certain vegetables, check with other gardeners. It may have been a poor growing season for that crop that year. If, however, most of the gardeners you know didn't have a problem, it may be that that vegetable just doesn't have the right growing conditions in your site and you should omit it or at least try a smaller patch the next time.

Kitchen Waste Nitrogen Sources

- beet greens and peels
- coffee grounds
- crab shells
- feathers
- fish scraps
- lobster shells
- milk
- mussels
- nutshells
- olive pits
- oyster shells
- peanut shells
- pine needles
- potato skins
- shrimp shells
- tea leaves

Note: When adding the above material to the garden or the compost heap, remember that the finer it is ground or chopped up, the quicker it will release its nutrients. Other commonly available materials you may have on hand that will contribute nitrogen are leaves of apple trees, all manures, dry seaweed, and raspberry leaves.

Distribution

No matter how good your planning and selection, you are still not producing a cash crop until you have a place to sell it. You have two alternatives: to sell it direct to the consumer or to sell it wholesale to the retailer. There are advantages and disadvantages in both methods.

Selling Direct

Selling direct means there is no middleman between you and the consumer. The roadside stand you buy from is often run by the farmer who is selling his own crops. Sometimes a local farmer will put up a stand just inside his stone wall or just off the road, with a sign on the nearest main road to direct people to him. The sign will usually say *Corn* or *Tomatoes* rather than advertising the name of the farm or the farmer. Sometimes local farmers are known locally and don't put up any sign at all. There used to be a wonderful farm in Westport, the town near me. The farmer sold turkeys, chickens, eggs, and just about every fruit and vegetable that could be grown in the area. There was no sign or any other indication of the location of the farm until you came right to the driveway. There the farmer had a sign that highlighted some of the produce available that day. There was always a long line of cars, and inside one of the outbuildings was a counter, complete with scales, where various members of the family would take turns waiting on the customers. Knowledge of the farm was spread solely by word of mouth, but that was all that was needed. Of course, this was a very large farm that also supplied many of the local markets.

If you want to sell this way, you can do it on a much smaller scale. Down the road a little way there is a family I have never met who every so often have something for sale. Sometimes their sign will say *Native tomatoes,* and there will be an old table with perhaps three dozen tomatoes arranged on it. Another time it will be flowers, and during the fall, usually grapes. Later on, the woodpile becomes visible and the sign is changed to *Firewood.* I do not know whether or not the business thrives, but the signs have been appearing for several years now, so it is obviously satisfactory to the homeowner.

If you want to put up a table and sell in this fashion, be sure your neighbors do not object. Rather than ask them directly, you might want to mention to each of them as you meet at the mailbox that you have so many whatever it is this year that you are "thinking of putting up a stand." If they are the kind of neighbors to object, they probably will quickly assume you are not kidding and you will get a reaction. On the other hand, if you are growing the right things, you may soon find that your neighbors will buy from you and spread the word among their friends, so that you are in business almost before you are ready.

Selling direct usually means that you do not need elaborate packaging. You will need a scale and paper bags of various sizes. The scale can come right out of your kitchen. The paper bags can be saved or bought wholesale; look in the Yellow Pages for a source near you. Your prices should be a little lower than those in the local market for the same produce, but do not feel you have to cut prices very much; your produce is fresher and probably more unusual than that in the market. Rather than sell too cheaply, add some personal touches. Put in thirteen ears of corn when someone buys a dozen— but be sure to mention that you are doing so or the customer will think you simply made a mistake. Heap your berry baskets high. Suggest recipes while you are wrapping if the customer seems interested.

The big disadvantage of selling direct is that you turn into a shopkeeper. A shopkeeper has long hours and cannot go fishing when the store is supposed to be open; you will have to be there whatever hours you initially set up. This can be very confining, especially if you do not really have much to sell and are not particularly interested in a full-time or full part-time (such as every afternoon) business.

The other problem is that business may be erratic: some days you may not have a minute to stop for lunch and other days you may not make more than one or two sales. You never know when someone will come, so you or a member of the family will always have to be available. Of course, you do not have to sit by the stand. A table bell that someone can push will alert you (if you can hear it in the house), or you can position the stand so that you can see it from the house and even hear if a car stops.

If you want to attract more business than that of your immediate neighborhood, and you probably will, you may have to put up a sign or two on the nearest main road, directing people to your little enterprise. The sign should have a name, preferably something with the word "farm" in it, and should be so arranged that you can change the specials. The specials can be as simple as *Vegetables and cut flowers* and as specific as *Vegetable spaghetti* and *Jerusalem artichokes*. You'll want to do some "copy testing" to see what descriptions attract the greatest number of customers, but that is fun. Keep a record of your sales results with certain wording on the sign, and you will soon see what works best. There is no doubt that "tomatoes" and "corn" are magic words, but if you are not growing them as cash crops, you can't benefit from their pulling power.

Selling Wholesale

One of the biggest disadvantages to selling wholesale is that you cannot sell at the retail price. This does not normally matter so much if you have a large quantity to sell, because the volume of your sales more than makes up for the smaller markup. On the other hand, selling wholesale is much less confining and can be done on a much more regular schedule. Once you have your customers, they will expect you at the same time each week, and you will know how much you are selling at each place and how much money you will bring home.

To sell wholesale you will have to make the rounds of the stores in your area that carry fresh produce. You may find that the small, nonchain stores are your best markets, because they have the freedom to buy wherever good produce appears. Some chains, however, give this freedom to their produce managers, so only trial and error and legwork will reveal all the possible outlets. Ask to speak to the produce manager in each store. He (I have never known a woman produce manager, but there must be some) is usually out in the department arranging vegetables or taking tired leaves off heads of lettuce, or else he is in the area behind doors just in back of the department supervising the packaging, checking incoming crates, and generally going about his business. When you ask where he is, ask his name and always use it in conversation with him; this will create a relationship more quickly than any other single thing you can do.

If you don't already have a thriving garden, discuss your project with him and listen carefully, making notes, to any suggestions. It sometimes takes a little time to warm managers up, but I find that they are generally very helpful people who like their work, take pride in their departments, and are happy to talk about them. If you already have surplus produce, ask the manager what he can use.

A good way to make a sale is to bring samples of what you want to sell; beautiful home-grown vegetables sell themselves.

Once you have made contact with produce managers, you will be able to do some of the work over the phone. When you have something to sell, you can just call a store and take orders over the phone, without having to make a trip to get an order and another one to deliver it. The stores will soon get to know the quality and dependability of your crops and will willingly give you orders in this way.

Do Not Oversell

In the beginning it is exciting to get orders, and the temptation will be to keep making the rounds. What I have in mind, however, is a comparatively small family garden that is just selling its extra produce. Unless you have been keeping track, you have no way of judging how many pounds of a given crop you are producing, and you may easily overestimate production. It is also important to decide how much time you are willing to devote to the business. My suggestion is that you start small, with a few stores as outlets, and gradually expand when you see how things go and how much you want to grow. It is important not to disappoint your customers, so do not make promises of deliveries until you have learned a bit more about the business.

If you find you can set up a regular delivery schedule, you might want to combine this with a regular phone call to check on what is needed in any week. The worst thing you can do is overstock your outlets; a large pile of ears of corn encourages buyers, but a large stack of shallots is neither necessary nor appropriate unless the area is rampant with gourmet cooks. The produce manager will know best, so the predelivery phone call will give him a chance to make any adjustments and save you the trouble of lugging down vegetables you may just have to lug back. Remember, the manager is also buying from wholesale markets, and he never knows absolutely what he will find in his trips to them, so he has to have a flexible buying pattern. The more you understand his problems, the better you will be able to sell to him.

Packaging

Packaging a product in America is so important that often—as with cosmetics—the package costs more than the contents. This is not so true in other countries, where people bring their own string bags to market and take loaves of bread home from the bakery without any bag or container.

Packaging produce prevents special problems, because the contents are sometimes delicate and because often the only way to sell them is to let people see what they are buying. The manager will advise you as to what he would like packaged. Usually Jerusalem artichokes, shallots, hot peppers, snow peas, leeks, and horseradish roots are sold packaged in trays with a plastic wrap. Raspberries and other berries need to be put in berry baskets and other containers. If you have a little money to invest in having labels printed (this can be done very inexpensively) with the name of your "farm' and a line that says your produce is organically grown and fresh-picked, you can then write in what the specific item is. Write clearly. The handwritten part will give it a personal, small-town touch. It will also save you money, because one label will do for all your products.

The trays and berry baskets can usually be bought very inexpensively, and sometimes you can get friends and neighbors to save containers for you; at the moment I have a garage full of berry baskets that I have saved over the years for some unrealized contingency—such as selling wild blackberries that grow freely in the area and are almost $3.00 a half-pint in the stores.

It wouldn't look natural to add ribbons and bows to most produce, but making hot pepper strings or garlic braids are acceptable ways of dressing up these vegetables. They are also devices that allow you to charge much more than the undecorated peppers or garlic would cost. Think creatively. If you are at all handy you can package your produce in the evening while watching television. It is much easier than you think. Sometimes company enjoys helping; you could have an old-fashioned party, like the old quilting or corn-husking parties. The produce managers are usually very receptive to ideas like this because it adds an interesting décor to their departments and helps set them apart.

Organic Crops

Organic crops bring higher prices, partly because they are considered more trouble and partly because they are rare. Throughout the book I have spoken only of growing things organically, and if you do, you should publicize the fact and get the benefit of it. More and more people are becoming aware that many of the pesticides and insecticides used on crops are not removed by washing or rinsing, and they would buy organically grown food if it were available. Health-food stores, of course, are prime markets and will help you in pricing organics (see what they charge). Health-food store managers are not quite as restricted in their buying, and their customers may be more adventurous in trying new things. There is probably at least one in your area; be sure to talk to the manager about selling your crops.

Pricing

The buyer in each store will have an idea of what he can sell your crops for; the price will vary from store to store and from week to week. Keep detailed records so you can see which are your best outlets, when is the best time of year, and the various other factors that will affect your profit. In the beginning you will have to take each manager's word for what is a fair price, but as your "brand" gains a reputation and an audience, you can begin to charge more. If your crops are especially beautiful and good-tasting, think of them as premium or deluxe and expect to get more for them than for run-of-the-mill items. In some communities the snob appeal sells higher priced items over lower priced ones, and yours should certainly fall into the former category.

The markup—the difference between what the store pays you and the price it asks the customer—will originally be set by the manager. As your produce becomes known and he comes to depend on you, as customers begin questioning him when he isn't stocking your vegetable spaghetti, for instance, you may be able to get him to settle for a lower markup. There are certain trade customs, however, and he will not budge below a certain point. You can find out what the going wholesale price is by reading some of the marketing columns in the paper; in discussing prices, the columnist will often give the wholesale price. Learn to translate "bushels" and other terms into "baskets" or "pounds" or whatever the form in which it reaches the consumer. If the manager consistently tries to buy from you at lower than the wholesale price, show him you know you are not getting a fair shake. Your produce is fresh, locally grown, and delivered to him already packaged; he should be paying you more, not less, than the wholesale price. Wholesale prices change weekly, sometimes oftener, so if you want to be very businesslike about this, you need to find a source for wholesale prices that you can refer to regularly.

6. Marketing Nonvegetable Crops

The gardening instructions I have given for lilies of the valley, daylilies, and similar common plants that are popular, marketable, and so prolific that they would be classified as weeds if they weren't so useful and so well liked will enable you to add to your spare income by selling cut flowers. If the demands of picking the flowers at the right time of day (usually early morning, when the dew is still on them), bunching them or combining them, and getting them to the market or the florist as soon as possible don't conflict with your schedule, and if flower growing appeals to you, you will definitely find a market for them. If you can create attractive arrangements, the local florists may even give you special assignments and furnish you with some of their plant material in addition to buying your own. Cut flowers may also be sold direct at your roadside stand, and in some ways this is a little less demanding than selling wholesale, but it is more time-consuming in terms of tending the stand.

Churches, special parties and functions, weddings, and many other local activities and local businesses such as restaurants all use cut flowers, and you could easily find that your entire cash crop will go to supplying flowers for all of these. The local florists may not welcome the competition, but business is business and I wouldn't consider that a minus. If you have a real talent for designing floral arrangements, you may find that watching the bride come down the aisle proudly bearing a bridal bouquet you designed gives you real satisfaction and pleasure as well as an excellent income.

You may also wish to think about selling plant material and potted plants or the edible crops derived from flowers. Pachysandra, for instance, continues to increase in price with no apparent diminution in popularity. It is commonly sold in flats, which you may have a collection of already. (If not, figure them into your selling cost.) The flats may contain as many as 100 plants or as few as 25; a visit to your local nursery will give you the going price in your area.

Flats are the usual way to sell ground covers and can be used successfully for English ivy, myrtle, and similar plant material. Shrubby plants that may have outgrown their site on your grounds and that you would like to sell, such as euonymus, should be potted, as should herbal ground covers, such as camomile.

Little Johnny-jump-ups self-sow themselves, and once you have a planting, you are set for life. Nothing is simpler than to pot the small seedlings that come up everywhere (even in the lawn) in the early spring. They bloom quickly and are ready for the market almost before you are. Since this type of potted flower is sold by both grocery stores and nurserymen, you can get a good start on cash from your garden with practically no work on your part.

Bulbs can be potted in the same way if they are strong-growing bulbs such as grape hyacinth or star-of-Bethlehem. Just wait until they show a small clump of green leaves, then pot and wait for them to bloom. You could probably sell them before they flower, but flowering plants always go faster and will bring more money. The trick in selling potted plants is having the patience to wait until they flower. With all those mentioned above, it isn't even necessary to pot the plant until it has started flowering or at least has a bud or two. Since you are selling something anyone with an inch of soil could grow himself, the only appeal is that they are buying something already in bloom.

As we have mentioned, some plant material is edible, such as daylily buds, which are described in the section on daylilies. On the other hand, some material must be dried. Japanese lanterns and bittersweet fall into this category. If you have a wooden beam in the garage or a wall into which you can put thumbtacks, drying is easy. Just gather your material, tie it loosely in a bunch, and hang it head down from a tack in the wall or beam. Unless you have a spell of exceptionally damp weather, the plants will dry themselves nicely and soon be ready to market. Take the time to tie them with a bit of colored wool (red or orange is effective) or ribbon (grosgrain rather than cotton) and pack them carefully, horizontally, in a carton.

If you are handy (and it doesn't take a great deal of skill), you can make wonderful wreaths out of almost anything you will find on your grounds and in woods and fields. Grapevines are the latest thing I have seen used for wreaths. They take a little working with before you get the hang of them, but they festoon trees and bushes all through many areas and can be had for the gathering. So if you spoil the first few wreaths, there's no harm done. Wheat or straw, gathered at strategic points around the wreath with a binding of any natural material you have handy, is also very popular and can be decorated with an occasional strawflower. Bittersweet also lends itself to wreath making, and the effect, with the orange and yellow berries, is very pretty. There is, however, a tendency for the berries to fall off, and I find this a more difficult kind of wreath to make than some.

Once you have started making wreaths, you will see possibilities in all sorts of plants and shrubs you never even noticed before. Remember that wreaths are no longer just for Christmas but are put on doors, walls, and even within the house during many seasons. They can be sold either direct or through a store or florist, and you should check the prices, because you may not realize how much the stores get for them. Of course, if you are selling wholesale, you must expect that your price to the store will be much less than the retail price.

Many flowers, such as dahlias, are very profitable when grown from seed. They are easy to grow and will flower profusely the very first season. The secret is to start them in the house, if possible, so that they are in bloom in time to sell for setting out in the spring garden. Potted dahlias, one to a pot, sell for as much as $3.50 each and are really easy to grow. They are understandably popular, and there is steady demand for them every year. The advantage to you of growing from seed instead of from the root is that you can sow many seeds in a small container; whereas if you are planting the roots, you can put in only one to a pot. On the other hand, you don't then have to transplant the roots to larger pots, and they will bloom earlier. They also command a higher price because they make bigger plants, but they cost more unless you have a good supply from your own garden (as you soon will after the first year of growing from seed). With dahlias, as with other plant material, your choice of how to go about it depends on your individual circumstances—how much room you have, whether you have room for starting seedlings indoors, and other relevant factors.

7. Think Small

If you have read up to this point, you now know all you need to know to get started. And no matter where you live—city street or country lane—you can pick cash crops that suit your circumstances. The city gardener has easier access to markets and less competition from garden-fresh produce and can ask higher prices; the country gardener has more room and more storage space both for garden supplies and crops. But both of you will be able to more than make up the expenses involved in gardening (supplies, fertilizer, tools) and to supplement your budget with cash in hand without having to be away from home. The working mother can make a little extra and still spend time with her children; husbands and wives will discover a hobby they can share and make money with at the same time; roommates can garden together or separately and divide the work (and the cash) accordingly; and singles will find their new occupation is an easy way to make new friends and acquaintances among fellow gardeners.

You cannot imagine how quickly enthusiasm for this project and the good feel of cash in hand will get you in over your head. Do not take on too much in the beginning; remember we didn't start out to do market gardening, we only wanted a little extra cash from surplus crops. You are bound to make a few mistakes in the beginning, and a small start will mean fewer mistakes. Until you feel confident with this new project, do not dig up another vegetable bed or send away for exotic flower seeds. If you do turn into a serious market gardener, you couldn't pick a better time to do it. The small farmer gets comparatively little for his crops; the cost of distribution and the profits of the distributor and retailer are what create the high prices you, the consumer, have to pay. But with a small operation, selling either direct or nearby, you can bypass all this expensive marketing structure and pocket the profit yourself. In addition, there has been a resurgence of farmers', or "green," markets, and it is now possible to rent, very inexpensively, small stands in large outdoor markets. If you find you are interested in enlarging your backyard business, write for a list of the names and addresses of the farmers' markets in your area; your state has a department that will give you that information. It will not pay you to get involved until you have committed yourself to growing much more than for your own table, but it may easily come to appeal to you after you have dabbled on a small scale for a while.

If you do decide to sell on a more ambitious level, plan for year-round sales so that you are not subject to the farmer's traditional dependence on the weather. A good crop of luffa can make up for a poor crop of garlic (although, on looking over the crops I have suggested, I see that most of them grow so fast and so easily that it is hard to imagine you will ever have real failures).

Cash-cropping is fun; it gets you out of the office or the house into the outdoors, and you need never feel guilty about letting household chores go, because you are, after all, working. And best of all, it's so easy. Mistakes take care of themselves: you can eat them or compost them—nothing is lost—and, like any farmer, you can blame your problems on the weather. Happy gardening!

Appendix A:
State Agricultural
Experiment Stations

ALABAMA

Cooperative Extension Service
Auburn University
Auburn 36830

ALASKA

Agricultural Experiment Station
University of Alaska
College 99701

ARIZONA

Cooperative Extension Service
University of Arizona
College of Agriculture
Tucson 85721

ARKANSAS

Cooperative Extension Service
University of Arkansas
Fayetteville 72701

CALIFORNIA

Agricultural Extension Service
University of California
College of Agriculture
Berkeley 94720

COLORADO

Cooperative Extension Service
Colorado State University
Fort Collins 80521

CONNECTICUT

Cooperative Extension Service
University of Connecticut
College of Agriculture & Natu-
   ral Resources
Storrs 06268

DELAWARE
Cooperative Extension Service
University of Delaware
College of Agricultural Sci-
ences
Newark 19711

DISTRICT OF COLUMBIA
Cooperative Extension
Service
The Federal City College
1424 K Street, N. W.
Washington, D.C. 20005

FLORIDA
Cooperative Extension Service
University of Florida
Institute of Food & Agricultural
Sciences
Gainesville 32601

GEORGIA
Cooperative Extension
Service
University of Georgia
College of Agriculture
Athens 30601

HAWAII
Agricultural Extension Service
University of Hawaii
Honolulu 96822

IDAHO
Cooperative Extension Service
University of Idaho
College of Agriculture
Moscow 83843

ILLINOIS
Cooperative Extension Service
University of Illinois
College of Agriculture
Urbana 61801

INDIANA
Cooperative Extension Service
Purdue University
West Lafayette 47907

IOWA
Cooperative Extension Service
Iowa State University
Ames 50010

KANSAS	Cooperative Extension Service Kansas State University College of Agriculture Manhattan 66502
KENTUCKY	Cooperative Extension Service University of Kansas College of Agriculture Lexington 40506
LOUISIANA	Agricultural Experiment Station Louisiana State University Agricultural College Baton Rouge 70800
MAINE	Cooperative Extension Service University of Maine College of Agriculture Orono 04473
MARYLAND	Cooperative Extension Service University of Maryland College Park 20740
MASSACHUSETTS	Cooperative Extension Service University of Massachusetts College of Agriculture Amherst 01002
MICHIGAN	Cooperative Extension Service Michigan State University College of Agriculture East Lansing 48823
MINNESOTA	Agricultural Extension Service University of Minnesota Institute of Agriculture St. Paul 55101
MISSISSIPPI	Cooperative Extension Service Mississippi State University State College 39762
MISSOURI	Cooperative Extension Service University of Missouri College of Agriculture Columbia 65201

MONTANA

Cooperative Extension
   Service
Montana State University
Bozeman 59715

NEBRASKA

Cooperative Extension
   Service
University of Nebraska
College of Agriculture & Home
   Economics
Lincoln 68503

NEVADA

Cooperative Extension
   Service
University of Nevada
College of Agriculture
Reno 89507

NEW HAMPSHIRE

Cooperative Extension
   Service
University of New Hampshire
College of Life Sciences & Ag-
   riculture
Durham 03824

NEW JERSEY

Cooperative Extension Service
Rutgers
College of Agriculture & Envi-
   ronmental Sciences
New Brunswick 08903

NEW MEXICO

Cooperative Extension Service
New Mexico State University
Box 3AE, Agriculture Building
Las Cruces 88003

NEW YORK

Cooperative Extension Service
Cornell University
College of Agriculture
Ithaca 14850

NORTH CAROLINA

Cooperative Extension Service
North Carolina State University
P.O. Box 5157
Raleigh 27607

NORTH DAKOTA

Cooperative Extension Service
North Dakota State University of Agriculture & Applied Science
University Station
Fargo 58102

OHIO

Cooperative Extension Service
Ohio State University
Agriculture Administration Building
2120 Fyffe Road
Columbus 43210

OKLAHOMA

Cooperative Extension Service
Oklahoma State University
201 Whitehurst
Stillwater 74074

OREGON

Cooperative Extension Service
Oregon State University
Corvallis 97331

PENNSYLVANIA

Cooperative Extension Service
Pennsylvania State University
College of Agriculture
323 Agricultural Administration Building
University Park 16802

RHODE ISLAND

Cooperative Extension Service
University of Rhode Island
Kingston 02881

SOUTH CAROLINA

Cooperative Extension Service
Clemson University
Clemson 29631

SOUTH DAKOTA

Cooperative Extension Service
South Dakota State University
College of Agriculture
Brookings 57006

TENNESSEE   Agricultural Extension Service
                                   University of Tennessee
                                   Institute of Agriculture
                                   P.O. Box 1071
                                   Knoxville 37901
TEXAS   Agricultural Extension Service
                                   Texas A & M University
                                   College Station 77483
UTAH   Cooperative Extension Service
                                   Utah State University
                                   College of Agriculture
                                   Logan 84321
VERMONT   Cooperative Extension Service
                                   University of Vermont
                                   State Agricultural College
                                   Burlington 05401

Appendix B: Free Seed Catalogs to Send For

If you have not discovered the world of seed and garden catalogs, you have a real treat in store. Bright with colorful photographs of flowers, vegetables, foliage plants, trees, and shrubs, they are also a storehouse of information. Many of them offer a wide range of garden facts and lore, and some even have excellent recipes. All offer plants as well as seeds and usually include planting instructions with an order. And best of all, they are free.

Once you have sent for a catalog, you will probably continue to receive it for two or three years even if you don't order anything from it. A few seedsmen will take you off the list the the season following the first year you fail to order, but you can always write again when you realize this has happened.

ARMSTRONG NURSERIES
P.O. Box 4060
Ontario, CA 91761

Specializes in fruits, fruit trees, and roses. Catalog in October.

BOUNTIFUL RIDGE NURSERIES
Box 250
Princess Anne, MD 21853

Specializes in berries, including the tayberry, which is a cross between blackberry and red raspberry. Also fruit, nut, and flowering trees. Catalog in November.

BRECK'S
6523 N. Galena Road
Peoria, IL 61362

Specializes in bulbs, which are shipped to you from Holland. Two catalogs: spring bulbs and fall bulbs. Spring-bulb catalog comes in September, fall-bulb catalog comes in January.

BURGESS SEED & PLANT CO.
905 Four Seasons Road
Bloomington, IL 61701

A general catalog: seeds and plants of vegetables, flowers, and fruits; trees and shrubs; houseplants. Catalog in January.

W. ATLEE BURPEE CO.
300 Park Avenue
Warminster, PA 18974

A must. Contains over 1,200 seeds, plants, trees, and shrubs; also new Burpee hybrids. Catalog in January.

COMSTOCK, FERRE & CO.
263 Main Street
Wethersfield, CT 06109

Good general catalog, well organized. Catalog in January.

DI GIORGI CO.
Council Bluffs, IA 51501

Packed with a wide range of items, with many varieties to choose from. Helpful planting information. Catalog in December.

J. A. DEMONCHAUX CO.
225 Jackson
Topeka, KS 66603

The nearest thing to ordering from France, this catalog offers gourmet vegetables in French and European varieties not found in other catalogs. Catalog on request.

GRACE'S GARDEN
Autumn Garden
Hackettstown, NJ 07840

If you want to grow the biggest vegetables, look here for the varieties to order. Many unusual offerings. Catalog on request.

GURNEY SEED & NURSERY CO.
Yankton, SD 57059

A delightfully busy catalog, with over 4,000 items, including chicks. Gurney's Gardening Magazine centerfold is full of information. Emphasis is on cold climate, hardy plant material. Catalog twice a year in December and August.

J. L. HUDSON, SEEDSMAN
P.O. Box 1058
Redwood City, CA 94604

A big catalog that is really fun to read because Hudson is a world seed service and you will come upon seeds for plants you never even knew existed. Especially good for cash-cropping if you have a market for unusual produce. Catalog on request.

JACKSON & PERKINS
Medford, OR 97501

Specializes in roses; beautiful photos. Also vegetable and flower seeds. Catalog in November.

JOHNNY'S SELECTED SEEDS
Albion, ME 14910

Emphasis is on cold climate, short-season gardening. Unusual seeds of fruits, vegetables, and herbs, with good organic growing information. Catalog in November.

J. W. JUNG SEED CO.
339 S. High Street
Randolph, WI 53956

Good old-time catalog. Comes in January.

KILGORE SEED CO.
1400 W. First Street
Sanford, FL 32771

Emphasis on warm-weather gardening, even Florida. Big on dwarf varieties for small gardens. Catalog in December.

KITAZAWA SEED CO.
356 W. Taylor Street
San Jose, CA 95110

Good source for Oriental vegetables. They are very helpful when you are looking for something you don't know the name of. Catalog on request.

MELLINGER'S, INC.
2310 W. South Range Road
North Lima, OH 44452

An awesome selection of about 4,000 items. Catalog in November.

NEW YORK STATE FRUIT TEST-ING COOOPERATIVE ASSOCIA-TION
Geneva, NY 14456

Highly specialized in fruits and fruit trees, items you won't see anywhere else. Catalog in September.

NICHOLS GARDEN NURSERY, INC.
1190 North Pacific Highway
Albany, OR 97321

Excellent catalog, not illustrated but full of rare and unusual herb, vegetable, and flower seeds. Growing information and good recipes a plus. A good source for Oriental and European vegetables. Catalog in November.

L. L. OLDS SEED CO.
Box 7790
Madison, WI 53707

A no-nonsense catalog that features old-time varieties often ignored by other growers. Corn, tomatoes, and berries your grandmother might have grown. Try their beefsteak tomatoes. Catalog in December.

GEORGE W. PARK SEED CO.
Greenwood, SC 29647

Very comprehensive catalog. Indoor gardening supplies as well as outdoor. Good midget varieties for the limited-space garden. Catalog in December.

R. H. SHUMWAY SEEDSMAN, INC.
628 Cedar Street
Rockford, IL 61101

Attractive catalog. Offers savings on bulk orders. Catalog in January.

STARK BROTHERS NURSERIES & ORCHARD CO.
Louisiana, MO 63353

Specializes in fruits, nuts, ornamental shrubs. Special catalog, adapted to climate, sent in some southern states. Catalog in December.

SUNRISE ENTERPRISES
P.O. Box 10058
Elmwood, CT 06110

An Oriental seed catalog; plant names and some other information in both English and Chinese. Seed packets very reasonably priced. Catalog on request.

THOMPSON & MORGAN
P.O. Box 100
Farmingdale, NJ 07727

A unique catalog of vegetable, fruit, and herb seeds. Confusing at first, but a little time spent browsing is fun and will soon show you how it is organized. Richly illustrated, full of unusual items, packed with growing information and sometimes nutrition information and recipes. Catalog in January.

TSANG & MA
1306 Old Country Road
Belmont, CA 94002

A rather mixed-up but interesting catalog of primarily Oriental seeds and cooking equipment, from steamers and woks to bamboo rice paddles and loofah scrubbers. Also non-Oriental vegetable seeds and herbs. Recipes with seed order. Catalog on request.

A Gardener's Guide and Glossary

This started out to be just a glossary, with a simple definition of terms, but I soon found that I wanted to include more information than is properly part of a glossary, so I have combined the glossary with a guide that can be used for quick reference. I hope you find it useful.

Gardening, like other specialized activities, has its own language. Many of the terms used in talking about gardening are technical; "damping off" and "friable" are examples that apply only to gardening. Some terms are self-explanatory, such as "ground cover" and "companion planting," even though you may want specific examples in order to apply them. But there are other words that you may think you know, only to find that they have a different meaning when used about gardening. One of the most difficult words in this category is "organic."

Originally, "organic" was applied to anything that was living or had once been alive. When I was a child I was taught that coal was organic because it had once been plants and trees, but stones were not because they had derived entirely from minerals and not from living matter. That definition has now been changed by organic gardeners. Today even *Webster's Dictionary* recognizes one meaning of organic as "relating to, produced with, or based on the use of fertilizer of plant or animal origin without employment of chemically formulated fertilizers or pesticides." If you think of "organic" and "chemical" as opposites, you won't go far wrong.

The following guide and glossary includes gardening terms used in the book, but I have also included some common gardening terms that you may encounter in other reading. I have tried to avoid the sometimes unwieldy preciseness of dictionary definitions in favor of everyday explanations, and I hope you find this helpful. Gardening, like cooking, goes more quickly and easily when you know your terms, but you should not need a degree in horticulture to understand what they mean.

ACID SOIL Acidity and its opposite, alkalinity, are measured on a scale of 1 to 10. This is called the pH scale. On the pH scale 7 is neutral and 6 is acid. The smaller the number, the greater the acidity. Since most vegetables will not thrive in acid soils below 6 on the pH scale (and some require soils in the alkaline range above 7), it is important to test your soil regularly for its pH. Acid soil is fine for certain plants, such as pachysandra, azaleas, and rhododendrons, but in general it is not desirable; 6.5 to 7 will accommodate most plants.

One way of creating an acid soil is through the use of mulches such as pine needles and oak leaves. If your soil is too acid, it is easily made more alkaline by the use of dolomite, crushed limestone, wood ashes, or ground oyster shells. It is not usually necessary to do this more than every three or four years.

AGRICULTURAL EXTENSION SERVICE The Department of Agriculture's agricultural extension service is the gardener's best friend. There is a branch in every state (I have included their names and addresses in Appendix A), just a phone call away from your garden. The branches are staffed by experts in every phase of knowledge concerning your grounds and gardening; they will tell you why your zucchini is wilting or what to do about black spot on roses. If you want advice on the best varieties of a vegetable to grow in your area, they will make recommendations. You can find out what plants are hardy in your zone and what problems are peculiar to your area. Extension-service staffers will even tell you what to do about an infestation of carpenter ants or how to safeguard yourself against desert snakes wandering into your garden. Ask them to send you a list of publications on gardening put out by the Department of Agriculture; if you allow for the fact that they are biased in favor of chemical gardening, you will find them very useful.

ALKALINE SOIL Alkaline soil is the opposite of acid soil and on the pH scale is represented by numbers from 8 to 10. As I have mentioned in the definition of acid soil, a neutral soil from 6.5 to 7 is the most generally useful. A too alkaline soil is just as bad as a too acid one; nothing will grow in it.

Many container soils become too alkaline because of bottom-watering; the salts rise to the surface and form a crust over the soil and on the rim of the container, rather than leaching out with the runoff of excess water. If you bottom-water your containers because it is more convenient, watch out for this condition.

In the in-ground garden, use the leaching method for a too alkaline soil; that is, water more than you need to for the crop. The excess salt will run off with the excess water. Of course, you will also lose some of the fertilizers, so these will have to be added in greater than normal quantity.

An easy way to correct a soil that is slightly too acid is to add peat moss and dig it in. This is inexpensive and has the added advantage of improving the texture of the soil.

ANNUAL To the gardener, "annual" means a plant that grows from seed, produces its flowers, fruit, and seeds, and then dies, all in one season. Annuals, however, are not the same in all parts of the country. If you live in a cold area you will grow many plants as annuals that a gardener in a warmer climate can grow as perennials. True annuals will live only one year no matter where they are grown.

Most vegetables, such as corn, tomatoes, lettuce, and potatoes, are annuals. A few, such as asparagus, rhubarb, and Jerusalem artichokes, are not and can be cropped for many years once they are established. Annual flowers include petunias, marigolds, and sweet peas.

APHIDS These garden and house-plant pests cluster on stems and leaves so thickly that they look like a furry coat. They can be removed by hand with a Q-Tip dipped in alcohol—the only way with house plants—or controlled with ladybugs (purchased from a dealer). Ladybugs are found just about everywhere, but they are commercially collected primarily in eight Western states, from where they are shipped all over the country. They are probably already in your garden but may not be in sufficient numbers to keep down the aphid population.

BEDDING PLANTS Bedding is used in the decorative sense; it is not a description of a truly separate group of plants. A bedding plant can be a low-growing shrub, a flower, a foliage plant, or even a vegetable. What makes it a bedding plant is its growth habit; it should be able to fill in and cover an area of the garden and sometimes should be compact in shape. Bedding plants are most commonly used in borders, where they form a solid mass lining the area at the edge of the bed. Examples of bedding plants include sweet alyssum, portulaca, candytuft, low-growing petunias, periwinkle, lettuces, coleus, and flowering cabbage. If what you want is a low-growing, compact plant, be sure you choose carefully among the various varieties. For example, look for dwarf forms of petunias and lettuces or you may be disappointed in the appearance of the finished bed.

BIENNIAL Whereas annuals require one year to flower and mature, biennials require two. Parsley, for instance, will not set seed until the second year, unlike radishes, which will seed at the end of the season. A biennial will die at the end of the second year.

Some biennials are treated as annuals. Parsley, for instance, is not a satisfactory herb for cooking the second year, so unless you want to let it continue growing in order to get your own seed, you would usually discard it after the first year. In practice I usually let a few plants of parsley, leeks, fennel, and similar biennials go to seed the second year and plant a new crop each season for the table. Since they would be in the way of rototilling if I left them in place, I usually transplant them in the fall to a more out-of-the-way spot. The leek flowers are attractive, similar to though not as showy or colorful as the alliums grown for their flowers, and could be kept in the flower bed.

BORON Boron is one of the trace elements essential to all living organisms, including humans. If your soil is deficient in boron, you may have a problem with beets, celery, and other vegetables. Organic gardeners usually do not have a problem with boron deficiencies.

BUCKWHEAT HULLS A pleasant mulch for the flower garden. Light and easy to handle, decorative in place, and an aid to the soil when, over the years, they work into it. Buckwheat hulls are available at many garden and farm centers; they may be in short supply in some areas because they are sometimes used by egg producers to pack egg cartons for shipment.

CALCIUM Calcium is essential for healthy plants just as it is for healthy humans. Lime and shells of various sorts are a good source. Adding calcium in the form of limestone is the easiest way to correct a too acid soil. Wood ashes and bonemeal are also good sources of calcium. Wood ashes are more easily available than they used to be because of the popularity of wood stoves; they can be stored indefinitely provided they are kept dry. Bonemeal is especially recommended for bulbs, but it is expensive.

CARBON Carbon makes up 50 percent of all organic matter and has many forms. Both diamonds and coal are forms of carbon; the graphite in your lead pencil is one form, and so is part of the gas that makes soda bubbly. It is necessary, in one form or another, for all living things. Chemical farming reduces the amount of the form of carbon known as carbon dioxide in the soil; a deficiency of soil-available carbon dioxide will reduce crop yields. A soil rich in organic matter will always be rich in carbon dioxide, and this is an argument for introducing your kitchen waste directly into your garden rather than composting it. If this is not feasible, however, composting is the next best thing.

CHEMICAL FERTILIZERS Chemical fertilizers are also referred to as artificial fertilizers, but actually this is misleading. A chemical fertilizer may be artificial, but it also may be a natural substance that has been processed in such a way that it is now artificial—that is, it does not occur that way in nature. Neither type of inorganic fertilizer is acceptable to organic gardeners. An example of this latter type of chemical fertilizer is superphosphate. In its natural state phosphorus is organic. It is often, however, combined with sulfuric acid to create superphosphate, and this is then considered a chemical fertilizer.

Chemical fertilizers that are factory-produced, as compared with natural rock bases that are combined with soluble chemicals (superphosphate), are lacking in trace elements. It is also possible that the combined fertilizers lose some trace elements in processing.

We have barely scratched the surface of knowledge of trace elements; it is only recently that we have been able to study any of them and to determine their importance to human health and nutrition. Only a few years ago zinc was not on the list of recommended dietary supplements at all. Today studies have shown that most Americans are deficient in zinc, and it is among the supplements commonly recommended.

Reliance on chemical fertilizers also tends to create soil that cannot renew itself. As plants take nutrients from the soil, organic matter plus soil bacteria form factories to produce more nutrients. Chemically fertilized soil offers nothing for soil bacteria to work with, and soon the soil becomes merely a holding medium, barren of useful bacteria, nutritious only to the extent that limited nutrients are provided by the chemicals constantly added to it.

If you use chemical fertilizers, keep an eye on your crop yield and your soil. Superphosphate and other chemical fertilizers that contain acid will increase soil acidity and will need to be limed oftener. Chemically fertilized soil should be mulched and mixed with compost in increased amounts.

Chemical fertilizers are much faster-acting than organic fertilizers and should be applied closer to the time when they will be needed by the plants.

CHLOROPHYLL Chlorophyll is the green coloring matter in plants that makes it possible for them to turn soil nutrients, water, sunlight, and air into food. It is an excellent deodorant, which is why it is used in candy mints to remove breath odors. If you run out of the mints, chew on a mouthful of parsley instead. Parsley is naturally high in chlorophyll and will cleanse the breath even of garlic and onion odors if eaten directly after ingesting these foods.

CHLOROSIS This is a disease caused by insufficient chlorophyll in a plant. It is easily recognized by yellowing of the leaves. Generally the addition of iron to the soil will correct the condition overnight. (If the application of iron does not correct yellowing of the leaves, consider the possibility of a nitrogen or magnesium deficiency.) Ask your garden center for an iron-rich fertilizer, preferably one that is chelated, and apply according to the directions on the package. For fast results, be sure to water it in after application.

Gardeners in fruit-growing areas where the soil may have been subjected to sprays of iron sulfate, iron oxide, or iron chloride should not use these materials in correcting chlorosis in their gardens. This is particularly liable to be the case where citrus is grown.

CLAY Clay is a type of soil, but it is not very desirable, and if you have clay soil, the first thing to do is to improve it.

You can determine whether or not your soil leans too much to the clay side by a simple test of its texture. Water a small area and scoop up a handful. Squeeze it. Clay will form a very compact ball. Drop it and it will break apart rather than crumble.

It is difficult to grow anything successfully in clay soil. The soil is hard for plant roots to penetrate and tends to stunt them. Water enters it with difficulty but is equally slow to drain, so that the roots may stand in water longer than is desirable. If you live in a cold area, clay will delay planting, because it is slow to warm up in the spring.

The best way to improve clay soil is to add organic matter in the form of humus, compost, or kitchen waste. Improving clay soil cannot be done overnight, and your best bet, if you have this condition, might be to go to raised-bed gardening with topsoil you bring in for the beds.

If you have clay soil, you should be extremely careful not to walk on it or work it when it is wet. It will compact into an impenetrable mass and you will never be able to restore it to a usable condition. This is another good reason to go to raised beds; you can then freely walk on your clay paths (although they may be slippery when wet) without affecting your plantings.

COMPANION PLANTING Plants, like people, like some of their neighbors better than others and, also like people, actually dislike some of them. If plants are placed in combination with neighbors they like, they will thrive; if placed near neighbors they dislike, they may not do at all well. Sometimes we know scientific reasons why certain plants seem to make good companions; often we have learned from observation that it is so without knowing why. It makes an interesting study, and any gardener, by careful observation and note-taking, may contribute to this knowledge.

Some vegetables that make good neighbors are peas and carrots, peas and bush beans, beets and kohlrabi, cabbage and beans, and tomatoes and parsley. On the other hand, vegetables that are not compatible and that should not be planted next to each other include tomatoes and fennel, tomatoes and kohlrabi (tomatoes seem to be fussy), and red and black raspberries. Sunflowers and Jerusalem artichokes don't get along with any other plants and do best off by themselves; the other plants are the ones to suffer, while the sunflowers and Jerusalem artichokes thrive blithely, unconscious of their companions. Even a bird feeder filled with sunflower seeds is hazardous to the health of a garden; nothing will grow under the feeder if the seeds are scattered around on the ground (by you or by the birds).

COMPOST Compost is the mark of a dedicated organic gardener, and it should appeal to you if you are a thrifty gardener because it's a real money-saver. Compost is any organic matter that is in the process of decaying. The end product is fertilizer, soil conditioner and recycling at its best. Unlike recycling of glass, metal, and paper, which often requires more energy than it saves, recycling of organic matter takes place all by itself. Left alone, it will all eventually return to the earth the nutrients it removed from it. With a little assist from you, it will do this fairly quickly, painlessly, and with an even better end product.

There are many ways to build a compost pile, but all start with saving all the kitchen wastes you normally throw away as garbage. This includes vegetable peelings, rinds, skins, seeds, cores, wilted and discarded fruits and vegetables, coffee and tea grounds, eggshells, cooked vegetables and other leftovers, the salad nobody finished, and anything else that is organic. Even fish and meat scraps can be included if you do not have a problem with animals getting into your compost heap. In addition, your grounds will provide leaves, grass clippings, and dead (but not diseased) weeds and plants from your garden. Layered with soil and manure, watered occasionally to speed decay, and turned over or aerated occasionally, your compost heap will soon be ready to furnish all the fertilizer and soil conditioner your heart desires. And all for free (you may even save money on garbage collection).

COPPER A trace element essential to a successful garden. Copper deficiency is not usually a problem, but your agricultural extension service office can tell you whether your area happens to be one of the few in which it is.

CROP ROTATION One way to cut down on garden problems is to plan your garden so that you do not grow the same vegetables in the same place each year. If you grow several crops a season, as you can easily do in the South, you will want to be especially careful. In the North, where you may have a summer and a fall crop, you may get away with the same garden plant one year but should arrange plants differently the next season. This is especially important for tomatoes, eggplant, and peppers and is good practice for all vegetables. Flowers and foliage plants do not seem to present the same problem.

Part of the reason for shifting things around is that different vegetables use up different nutrients, and changing off for a couple of seasons gives the soil a chance to replenish what has been drawn on the most. Another reason is that insects and diseases get set on a certain area and will tend to return and recur if you grow one thing too long in the same spot. Large-scale farmers resort to extra-heavy fertilization and spraying to overcome this, but their crops are very vulnerable, and many agricultural experts think that one-crop farming will one day lead to disaster.

Keep all your garden plans, and eventually you will be able to go back to your original one and then just follow, year by year, the ones you had worked out. You may improve on them through experience, but you won't have to design from scratch unless you want to.

CUTTINGS Taking cuttings from an established plant is an easy way to propagate many crops. My mother does it even with tomatoes, but I would suggest it for pachysandra and other ground covers, roses, and similar bushes, and many flowers, such as hyacinth, African violets, begonias, and gloxinia. Cuttings also work well with many herbs, such as watercress and oregano.

There are many kinds of cuttings, softwood and hardwood, stem and leaf. It is a free way to increase your stock and a fascinating part of gardening.

CUTWORMS When you are digging in your garden, especially in the spring, you may come upon small fat "worms" that curl up if you touch or disturb them. They grow from eggs laid by cutworm moths, usually during the fall, in weeds and grass. Kill them when you see them, but assume there are many you will never see. Cutworms damage young seedlings by cutting the stem off just above the soil line. They seem most attracted to tender, newly set transplants of tomatoes and peppers.

Cutworms are easily controlled. When setting out young seedlings, place a collar of foil or cardboard around the stem, about an inch into the soil and two inches above it. Put the collar on loosely so it does not bind the plant, but be sure it surrounds the stem completely. In addition, you can scatter a ring of wood ashes around the plant, wetting them down after spreading. If you have a garden toad, make him welcome; cutworms are his favorite food.

DAMPING OFF Damping off is a name used for a disease of young seedlings that is caused by various organisms but in all cases causes the death of the seedlings. I have never seen it happen in in-ground sowings, but it is a common problem with flats of seedlings that are sown indoors to get a start on the season. The first you will know of it is when you check your flats some morning and find patches of seedlings that have apparently toppled over because they have become too weak to stand up. You can try carefully removing the affected seedlings with a pair of tweezers and dusting the soil with a mixture of powdered charcoal and vermiculite. The charcoal should first be heated in the oven to make sure it is sterile, and the vermiculite should be taken from a fresh bag. This may or may not work; in any case, affected flats should be isolated from the rest of your flats.

There are certain garden practices to follow that will help prevent damping off. First and most important is to use a sterilized planting medium: vermiculite, sand, or sterilized potting soil, as well as a combination of the three, will all do. Next, sow your seeds thinly enough to give them air and room to grow; overcrowding seems to favor damping off. Finally, do not keep the planting medium too wet, and never leave the flat in standing water. It is assumed, of course, that you are also following the usual rules for growing seedlings: plenty of light, plenty of air, and an atmosphere neither too hot nor too cold. In addition, all planting containers, whether flats or pots, must be thoroughly cleaned before using; I always put a few drops of chlorine bleach in soapy water and scrub with a brush before rinsing in clear water; it is years since I have lost any seedlings to this discouraging disease.

DUST MULCH Mulch is generally thought of as a layer of organic material spread over the garden suface. Dust mulch requires nothing to be added; it converts the soil surface to a layer of "dust" which helps retain the moisture already in the soil, instead of allowing it to be lost through surface evaporation.

A dust mulch is easily made; frequent, shallow cultivation of the soil when it is dry will quickly reduce it to the desirable texture. Dust mulches are liable to blow away during very windy weather, and, of course, they do not have the advantage of other types of mulches of adding organic matter to the soil. They do look very neat, however, and do keep down weeds most effectively.

FLAT A flat is a shallow container of wood or plastic with sides about 3 inches high. The most common size is about 14 inches square. Nurseries and garden centers use them both to hold seedlings and to hold small containers of seedlings. If you buy a flat of seedlings, you get to keep the flat. If you buy small containers of seedlings, you will usually be asked to take them separately and to leave the flat. Obviously, therefore, it is difficult to acquire flats in the beginning, but they are very useful and you should save any you may get.

Flats are designed especially for growing seedlings and, even when full, are not too heavy to move. They provide enough room for soil and have excellent drainage. It is not necessary to put a layer of gravel or other drainage material in a flat; it can be filled completely with the growing medium.

FORCING "Forcing" is the term used to describe the various processes by which plants can be tricked into growing or flowering faster than their normal cycles. The early azalea plants and other flowering plants in the local florist shops have been forced into bloom in order to tempt winter-weary consumers, and they command a much higher price because of the extra work involved and because they are out of season. The thrifty gardener may well want to learn how to force various cash crops in order to capitalize on this lucrative market.

Since each plant has its own growth cycle, it is necessary to learn how to force each one in which you are interested. The easiest to start with are the spring bulbs, which can be forced in individual pots to create an array of hyacinths, daffodils, crocuses, and grape hyacinths that will sell as quickly as they are offered. Do not, however, limit yourself to flowers. The section on rhubarb tells how to force this vegetable for preseason sales, and you will soon discover that there are many other ways to be an early-bird gardener.

Forcing also applies to branches of flowering crab apple, dogwood, and forsythia that are sold in florist shops long before the outdoor trees and shrubs are in bloom. The woodier the plant, the longer it will require to force it into bloom. Pussy willows, on the other hand, will force in less than ten days. The closer the plant is to its normal blooming time, the more quickly it can be forced into bloom.

Branches or cuttings for forcing are best taken around noon, when the temperature is above freezing, the milder the better. If the stem is very woody, crush it so that it will more readily absorb water.

Know your market. If you live in an area where flowers and flower arrangements are good sellers, you may find that forcing unexpected plants, such as branches from birch, maple, or willow, will produce interesting plant materials that lend themselves to unusual arrangements. Experimenting will lead to some agreeable and profitable surprises.

FRIABLE Friable means easily crumbled and refers to the texture of soil that is in good condition. If you pick up a damp handful of soil, squeeze it, and then try to break it up, it will crumble into small particles. Clay soil will stay in a tight ball or break apart into large pieces; sandy soil will run through your fingers. Soil that is rich in decomposed organic matter will crumble.

The importance of friable soil is that it provides support for roots without being too difficult for them to penetrate; it is the ideal growing medium for mature plants.

GERMINATE Germinating is the act of beginning to grow; the first tiny sprout that forms a bump on the seed is a sign of germination. No matter how excellent your seeds, not all will germinate, and those that do not can be discarded. When sowing seeds—before you know how many will germinate—you always need to sow more than you want to end up with. This is not a scientific process but a guess, which is why thinning out is usually necessary after all the seedlings have developed.

Keeping a garden record that includes the rates of germination of seeds from various sources can save money the following season. Some seed houses seem to have better seeds than others, and the rate of germination, or what percentage of seeds germinate, is one way of judging the quality of the seeds.

Seeds do not all germinate in the same length of time. If you know this, you will not think something is wrong when your parsley seeds show no sign of life two weeks after they have been planted. Radish seeds are very quick to germinate, carrots take longer, and parsley takes several weeks. Be patient and keep a journal so you will know what to expect the next time.

GREEN MANURE Small gardens do not usually lend themselves to green-manuring, but you have probably encountered the term in your reading of garden books and may want to know more about it. Manure usually refers to material spread on top of the soil or incorporated into it; green manure refers to plants grown in the soil and then plowed into it because of their ability to replenish, rather than deplete, soil nutrients. If ever you found yourself in a position in which you could not have a garden but wanted to keep that area for future gardening use, planting a crop of green manure would be a good thing to do. Gardens should never be left bare, and green-manure crops, once they are sown, need no further attention. They are even better for the soil than compost and include nitrogen-fixing plants, whereas compost uses up nitrogen as it decomposes.

Most of the green-manure plants are legumes. These include alfalfa, black medic, and cowpea, which will grow anywhere in the United States; alsike clover, wood's clover, and field brome grass, which grow in the North; Alyce clover, Austrian winter pea, and crotolaria, which grow in the South; and even some, such as berseem or Egyptian clover, that will tolerate the desert alkaline soil of the Southwest when grown under irrigation.

GROUND COVER This term refers to plants with the common characteristic of covering the ground. They are all easy to grow, spread without any effort on your part, and are generally decorative. Ground-cover plants are problem solvers. They grow in that shady spot under the trees where lawn will not; they form attractive borders around the house or garage; they are forgiving of soil and do well in urban gardens as well as on country estates. They will even do well in window boxes, filling in the spaces left between the geraniums.

Ground covers are good cash crops because there is a constant demand for them. Since they propagate themselves, there is always a ready supply, and they are easy to transplant into flats or containers. Among the most popular ground covers are pachysandra and myrtle (periwinkle). English ivy is a favorite with apartment dwellers and penthouse gardeners, and the common violet and evergreen sedums are welcome in city or country.

HARDENING OFF When plants are grown indoors for any length of time, as when you start seedlings in early spring, they must be conditioned before they can be permanently set out; this conditioning process is called hardening off. Hardening off allows the plants to adjust gradually to the outdoors. This can be done by putting them in a cold frame and gradually increasing the exposure to open air. Another way is to put them out during the warm part of mild days, remembering to take them in before the afternoon turns cooler. An exact hardening-off schedule cannot be given because it depends on the weather, which may turn unexpectedly cool even fairly late in the season. If you are anxious to set out your plants but concerned about a possible cold spell, hedge your bets with cloches or similar coverings that can be put over the plants during the night or on an especially cold or windy day and removed when the weather is temperate.

Some plants are much more tender than others; eggplant and peppers, for instance, are very sensitive to cold. Many plants, such as lettuces, leeks, and radishes, are fairly hardy and will survive even a light frost.

HARDINESS ZONES The U.S. Department of Agriculture has divided the United States into ten zones according to the approximate range of average annual minimum temperatures for each zone. To make it easy for you to determine in what zone your area falls, the USDA has prepared a Plant Hardiness Zone Map that shows at a glance the determination for each section of the country. Most seed packets indicate the coldest zone in which the contents can be planted, and garden books generally discuss crops in these terms. The map is available free from your Agricultural Extension Service office.

HARDPAN If you have ever dug a moderately deep trench in your garden, you have probably noticed that the earth is layered; the top layer is probably topsoil, and below it the earth becomes lighter in color and less rich in nutrients. Often builders strip off the layer of topsoil during construction and put infertile subsoil on top when leveling the land off after building has been completed. If this happens, you may have great difficulty in establishing a lawn or growing anything but weeds.

Among the layers that may exist in the soil is one that is not only infertile but also impervious to water; this is called hardpan. It may occur six inches below the surface or four times as deep, but wherever it exists, it is bad news for plant life. Hardpan is more liable to occur where the soil is clay.

Hardpan layers cut off the topsoil from the subsoils and make it difficult for plant roots to penetrate to the subsoil, leading to shallow-rooted plants deprived of nutrients. Water falling on soil with a hardpan layer may either run off too quickly or puddle. If you suspect hardpan is causing garden problems, apply to your Agricultural Extension Service and they can find out for you.

HEEL IN Heeling in is a way of keeping plants alive and healthy when you do not have time to plant right away. This situation may arise when you have ordered plants, such as small trees, shrubs, or bushes from a nursery, and they arrive at an inconvenient time. Berry bushes, asparagus roots, and rhubarb plants are all plant material that you may order in quantity; if you cannot plant them immediately upon arrival, they may dry out and die. The solution is to heel them in by digging a shallow trench, laying the plants in the trench, and covering the roots with soil. Once they are completely covered, water thoroughly. The plants can be put close together; you are not planting them, only protecting them against drying out. When you are ready to plant, dig out a few at a time.

HUMUS Humus is decomposed organic matter. Forest soil under the layer of leaves is humus, as is part of a mature compost pile. It has a uniform, fairly fine texture and is very valuable for the garden.

Many gardeners mistakenly assume that all black soils are humus; this is not so. While humus is always dark brown or black, not all dark soils are fertile, and many black, mucky soils that look rich are not. In the Florida Everglades, for example, the soil is practically black, but an attempt to use it to grow cabbages was unsuccessful because it lacks essential nutrients. Obviously, since the Everglades is not a desert, the soil will support some forms of plant life, but it would not be a good place to put a vegetable garden.

HYBRID Hybrids are plants that have been developed by man through cross-fertilization. They arise from an attempt to breed plants with more desirable characteristics. Disease resistance is one characteristic that has been developed in many hybrids, including roses, tomatoes, and berries. Colors not found in nature, larger blooms, dwarf size or giant size, and other changes have all been developed through cross-fertilization.

Not all hybrids are an improvement; a case in point is the "plastic" tomato, which was bred to travel well and stand up under the rigors of modern transportation and storage methods. This type of tomato is considered a success by the marketeer but not by the consumer. It is not worth buying or eating, because in the process of hybridization all the worthwhile qualities of a tomato—its flavor, texture, and general deliciousness—have been lost.

If you like to gather your own seeds, hybrids may present a problem. Many are sterile and will not set seed—this is especially noticeable in certain varieties of petunias—and others will prove a disappointment because they will not come true to variety the next season.

INTENSIVE GARDENING Intensive gardening is any method that increases crop yield over what row gardening would produce. The usual method of planting in neat rows, which was customary until fairly recently, left a great deal of unused, and therefore wasted, growing area. Commercial farmers, unfortunately, must still plant in rows in order to use farm machinery.

There are many ways to garden intensively. The French method was the first to be adopted in this country, but it requires a great deal of preparation and work on the part of the gardener. The Chinese method is less labor-intensive and relies primarily on raised beds that are scatter-sowed; it forms the basis of most intensive gardening practiced today.

Anything that utilizes more garden space for crop production could rightfully be called intensive gardening. This includes minimizing the area given over to paths by planting in beds that are about five feet wide—therefore reachable from the sides without the necessity of a path through the bed; sowing the seeds broadcast over the bed instead of in neat rows; growing up fences or supports wherever possible; replanting as soon as a crop is harvested if the weather will allow another crop; and growing vegetables in tandem when one will mature before the other is crowded by its companion crop.

Intensive gardening makes good sense, and it is easy to get the knack of it. A fringe benefit is less work for the gardener, because the crops grow so thickly that weeds are minimized. It is especially good for the urban gardener or for anyone who must garden in containers because it makes the most efficient use of whatever soil area is available.

IRON An important nutrient for the formation of chlorophyll and for healthy plants. It is usually sufficiently abundant for normal plant requirements but may need to be supplied to acid-loving plants, such as blueberries, azaleas, and pachysandra. Lack of it results in a yellowing of the plant foliage. Chelated iron fertilizers—available in garden centers—may be applied, and incorporating more humus into the soil is a good long-term corrective.

KELP Kelp is a common brown seaweed that can be gathered on the beach and used as garden fertilizer. If you are not near a source of it, you can buy fish and seaweed fertilizers in garden centers. Kelp is particularly rich in potassium and contains appreciable amounts of nitrogen and phosphorus.

LEACHING Leaching is the process whereby soil nutrients are carried down out of the soil into the subsoil or, in the case of potted plants, into runoff water. If there is excessive rainfall or excessive watering of container plants, the result will be a deficiency of nutrients unless a greater than usual amount of fertilizer is added.

LEAF MOLD The rich black humus that lies under the leaves in the forest is leaf mold. If you have leaves available in the fall, you can make your own leaf mold by composting it. Since most leaves are somewhat acid, however, it is advisable to add lime, unless you are reserving the leaf mold for acid-loving plants. Shredding the leaves, either with a lawn mower or a shredder, will speed up the formation of leaf mold.

Leaf mold is especially useful in dry areas or in urban gardens where soil texture may be poorer, because it improves soil texture; it will hold up to ten times as much moisture as will ordinary topsoil. Used freely in containers, it will substantially reduce the chore of frequent watering.

LIME Lime, made from ground limestone, is the simplest and easiest way to correct soil acidity. It is available in bags at all garden centers and keeps indefinitely in a dry place.

The only sure way to determine whether your lawn or garden needs liming is through a soil test, which you can make yourself with a kit or have done by the Agricultural Extension Service in your state.

MAGNESIUM Magnesium is an essential trace element; without it, plants cannot utilize other important nutrients, such as phosphorus and nitrogen. If your garden is deficient in magnesium, the leaves on the bottom parts of the plants will turn yellow. This can occur gradually, starting with the edges of the leaf and progressing toward the center, until all of the leaf except the veins has lost its green color. Eventually the yellow will turn to brown and the leaf will die. If you have a compost heap, you will probably never have a problem with magnesium deficiency, since carrot tops, grasses, and leaves are among the common sources of magnesium.

MANGANESE Manganese is a minor but important element that only recently has been recognized as essential to plant growth. Some soils are naturally deficient in manganese (the Agricultural Extension Service can tell you if this is true of the soil in your area), and some are made deficient by too heavy liming. If you use manure to fertilize and mulch your garden, you never need worry, because it is rich in manganese.

MANURE Most gardeners are aware that well-rotted horse manure is excellent for the garden, whether added to the compost heap, dug into the topsoil, or used as a mulch. You may not know, however, that cattle, rabbit, chicken, sheep, and other manures are also valuable. The Chinese also use human waste, which they call night soil, but this may create certain problems and is not recommended in the United States.

There has long been an argument as to whether the value of manure lies primarily in its ability to improve soil texture or whether it actually is a fertilizer. Recent studies in Japan would seem to prove that it is an excellent fertilizer; crops grown with large applications of manure produced more and better vegetables than crops grown without manure.

If you live in the city, you may feel that manure is not available to you, but actually it is; it comes dried and in bags. The bags come in various sizes and are light to carry. Like well-rotted manure, dried manure has no odor and will not bother even the most squeamish gardener.

MULCH Mulch is material that covers the soil of the garden, between plants, so as to kill the weeds and conserve moisture. It can be organic, such as leaves, grass clippings, manure, hay, or seaweed, or inorganic, such as black plastic. Whatever you use, it will save the enormous amount of time that the unmulched garden requires to weed and water.

Black plastic will take more time to put down, but it can be used for several seasons. If the cost bothers you, you can spread thick layers of newspapers instead and cover with a thin decorative layer of organic material. This might be an inexpensive solution for city gardeners. Sometimes you can get black plastic free; if you know an architect, ask him to save the black plastic wrappings from his blueprint paper.

If you use organic material, it will not only keep down the weeds and save water, it will also improve the soil and add nutrients. A compost heap gets so hot in the process of decomposition that it kills all the weed seeds. If you use grass clippings direct from the lawn, you may have a weed problem unless you put it down in a very thick layer. Ideally, a mulch of organic material should be at least six inches thick.

NITROGEN Among the major fertilizers, and by far the most expensive, is nitrogen. It is the first number in the 10–10–10, 5–10–5, or similar designation on your big bag of fertilizer. Each major fertilizer has its own area of importance; nitrogen is essential for good leafy top growth. This means that you need more of it if you are growing lettuces, spinach, beet greens, kale, and cabbages. Unfortunately, it is quicker than other nutrients to leach out of the soil and needs to be replenished oftener during periods of heavy rain. This also applies to container gardening, since you may tend to water leafy vegetables oftener and may not realize the need of adding more nitrogen.

The numbers on the fertilizer package help you determine whether that fertilizer is suitable for your crop. If you are growing a lot of leafy crops, the first of the three numbers should always be 10 (as in 10–5–10). If you don't want to use a mixed bag of fertilizer but want to add just nitrogen, its sources are cottonseed meal, dried blood, and bonemeal. If you're a city gardener, your town may offer free treated sewerage sludge; a plastic bag of this is not unpleasant to use and is an excellent source of nitrogen.

The nitrogen content listed on a bag of fertilizer can make you a smarter shopper. Since it is the most expensive ingredient listed, you can compare prices in terms of the percentage of nitrogen in the bag. If the price is higher for a bag with a smaller percentage of nitrogen, it is not a good buy.

NUTRIENT Nutrients, in the gardener's vocabulary, are anything plants can utilize to further their growth. Strictly speaking, these are elements such as nitrogen, phosphorus, potassium, and the trace elements, but generally water and often sunlight are also included. Studies have shown that soils that are deficient in essential nutrients produce plants that are also deficient. If the plants are edible and part of our diet, we are being deprived also. This is one of the dangers of extensive use of chemical fertilizers, because they do not contain—man does not even know about—all the essential trace elements that are naturally found in organic matter.

ORGANIC Anything that is in its natural state—that is, as it occurs in nature. Nothing that is processed is organic, although it may have started out as a natural product. Organic fertilizers do not have anything artificial added. In contrast, chemical fertilizers are man-made, either by combining an organic fertilizer with a chemical (as in superphosphate, which is phosphorus to which sulfuric acid has been added) or by developing them in a laboratory from materials such as petroleum.

Since most chemical fertilizers are petroleum-based, their price tends to reflect the price of oil. In recent years they have become increasingly costly. You can make some of your own organic fertilizer cost-free from kitchen wastes. It is possible to save money and improve your gardening practices at the same time. You can also then market your crops as organically grown, which commands a higher price for them.

PEAT MOSS Peat moss is organic material in an advanced stage of decomposition. It is a valuable garden material for a number of reasons: it will improve the texture of both sandy and clay soils; it will increase the moisture-holding capacity of the soil—peat can absorb fifteen times its dry weight in water; and it adds some nutrients, depending on the plants of which it has been formed. It will make an alkaline soil less so and will create an acid soil for blueberries and other acid-loving plants.

Peat moss can be used as a mulch, but I would not advise it, because it will totally absorb a light rainfall, so that none of the moisture will reach the soil, and, if applied in any depth, is liable to form a crust from which water will simply run off.

PEAT POTS Peat pots are, not surprisingly, made from peat pressed into flowerpot shapes. They are very useful for sowing seeds, especially when individual plants are wanted, such as dahlias or tomatoes. Their big advantage is that no transplanting is required, and therefore the plants are not shocked by being moved during a critical stage of their growth. The plants can be put directly into the ground or container without being removed from the peat pot. If this is done, the edges of the pot should be broken down so that they are below the surface of the soil, and the plant should be thoroughly watered. Peat pots come in a number of sizes, are inexpensive, and store well.

PERENNIAL Perennials are plants that continue to bloom year after year once they are established. Many of them will have growth cycles of good years and poor years, but others will do equally well year after year. If you find your favorite perennials take every other year off, you might try a second planting to see if you can fill in the alternate poor years with the second group.

PERLITE Perlite is a soil conditioner that is sold by the bag in garden centers; the white particles you see in some potting mixtures are perlite. If you have house plants and make your own potting mixtures, you probably already use perlite to keep your container soil from compacting. It is sterilized and can be used, like vermiculite, as a seed-starting medium. It is much too expensive for in-ground gardening use and should be kept for container gardening.

PESTICIDES Chemicals used for controlling pests. Gardens are naturally subject to a number of pests, and some gardeners are quick to reach for the spray gun as soon as they see signs of anything amiss. Many pests will go away by themselves or will be controlled by natural enemies if you leave them alone long enough for their natural enemies to find them.

Organic gardeners are very careful not to use most chemical pesticides and rely instead on a strong spray from the garden hose or on kitchen items such as salt and cayenne pepper to free plants from most pests.

pH A measurement of soil acidity or alkalinity, also known as soil reaction. *See also* acid; alkaline.

PHOSPHORUS Phosphorus is the second ingredient listed on bags of fertilizer; the 5 in 10–5–10, for example, refers to the phosphorus content. Phosphorus acts as a catalyst; it makes everything else work. It is essential to base root development and to good fruit set, and without it plants cannot have strong stems.

A sign of too little phosphorus is usually to be seen in the leaves, which will yellow or develop a purplish tinge.

POTASSIUM Potassium is the last fertilizer listed on the bag in the formula, such as 10–5–10. Also known as potash, it is one of the three major fertilizers. It acts like antifreeze, making plants winter-hardy and enabling them to stand low temperatures. If you like to leave root crops in-ground for winter harvesting, they need potassium to see them through. Root crops need more potassium than other vegetables, but all plants need it to a considerable extent. If by any chance your soil is too rich in nitrogen, potassium has the ability to counteract this excess and can help restore proper soil balance. Wood ashes are an excellent source of potassium; greensand, available in garden centers, is another.

POTTING SOIL When gardening in containers, whether you are doing large-scale terrace or penthouse gardening or kitchen-windowsill gardening, special attention must be paid to the soil in the containers. Not only will not any soil do, you cannot even take good garden soil and use it as is. Potting soil has been the object of much study, and scientifically researched mixes are now available.

The best potting-soil mix is the one developed by Cornell University, known as Cornell Mix. You can buy it by the bag in garden centers, where it is sold under a number of names, such as Jiffy Mix, Redi-Earth, and Pro-Mix. If you cannot find those particular brands but think something else is Cornell Mix, check the list of ingredients. The mix should be basically vermiculite, peat moss, and fertilizers. This mix can be used as is, but you will get a better crop if you adapt it by adding more of the ingredient that the plants in a container particularly require: for example, more phosphorus and potassium for root vegetables, nitrogen for leafy vegetables. In addition, the extension service recommends a weekly application of a solution of liquid fertilizer—fish emulsion is good—according to how much you are watering, how fast the plants are growing, and what the recommended rate is on the package.

These ready-made mixtures are a boon to the city gardener because they are handy and easy to store. They are, however, more expensive to buy premixed than if you mixed your own. This can be done by combining a bushel of peat moss, a bushel of vermiculite, one 3-inch flowerpotful of lime, and two 3-inch flowerpotsful of rock phosphate and mixing thoroughly. If you live in the country, this can be premixed and stored in the garage so it is always handy; it will keep indefinitely.

An additional advantage to using this type of potting soil is that it is lightweight. The chore of moving containers around, whether to water or to take them in or out of the sun, is considerably lessened.

PRUNING Pruning is the human way of improving on nature by controlling unrestrained growth. It is simply cutting off part of the plant to shape it, to remove dead or diseased portions, to increase root growth, or to improve the health of the plant. Some plants, such as roses and forsythia, can be pruned quite severely to their advantage; others, like fruit trees, must be pruned judiciously or the trees will be irretrievably damaged. Bonsai, the Japanese art of dwarfing trees, depends largely on root pruning, a very specialized skill. Pinching—squeezing off buds or the ends of branches between the thumb and forefinger—is a form of pruning.

RAISED BEDS Raised beds are a form of intensive gardening in which the growing area, or bed, is raised higher than the rest of the garden, such as paths and storage areas. Both the French and the Chinese methods of intensive gardening use raised beds. A raised bed can be edged with a wood frame of boards or railroad ties and filled with a good friable soil rich in humus and manure. One advantage of a raised bed is that you are not stuck with the soil your grounds come with. Another is that a raised bed can be constructed in an urban garden—on a rooftop or on a terrace, by making it deeper and constructing a base for each bed—or in your in-ground garden. A practical, though not particularly decorative, way of making small raised beds is to use tires that have been turned inside out to contain the soil. It is possible to construct a raised bed without a frame, but the edges may erode and will have to be rebuilt every so often; there will also be greater loss of moisture with this method. Raised beds are a boon to the handicapped or to a gardener with a back problem, because they require less bending, or even no bending at all, depending on how high they are raised.

ROTOTILLING Rototilling is simply digging up and turning over the soil with a machine called a Rototiller. In the country you can usually find someone with a Rototiller to come in and do the job for you if you do not want to invest in or handle the equipment yourself. A Rototiller comes in various sizes, and only the large ones will do much more than break up the soil surface. After rototilling, it will be necessary to pick over and discard large stones and to rake the surface. If you rototill, do it either in the fall or just before the planting season; it could be an easy way to dig in fertilizer and compost.

SIDE-DRESSING Side-dressing is a way of adding fertilizer to growing plants. It is done by laying a bead of fertilizer down along both sides of the plant row or in a circle around large individual plants. If you garden intensively, this will not work and you will have to scatter-sow the fertilizer, first holding aside the leaves of the plants. Be careful not to overfertilize with this method and not to let fertilizer touch plant stems.

SPAGHNUM MOSS *See* peat moss.

SUPERPHOSPHATE Organic rock phosphate that has been converted to a chemical fertilizer by the addition of sulphuric acid.

TENDER A term used to describe plants that are especially sensitive to cold. Tender plants cannot be set outdoors until all danger of frost is past and the ground has warmed up.

THINNING OUT The act of removing an excess of seedlings so that the ones left are not crowded and have good air circulation. Beginning gardeners resist thinning out because they are reluctant to discard what seems like perfectly good plant material, but more experienced gardeners know that crowded plants will not be healthy or productive. In some cases, as with lettuce or beet-top thinnings, you can wait a little until the excess plants have matured slightly and can be eaten. If they are very crowded, thin in stages and eat the last crop of thinnings.

It is sometimes possible to avoid having to thin by sowing seeds more thinly. This is comparatively easy with beet seeds, which are large, if you realize that each beet seed contains three plants and will invariably have to be thinned a little. Beet greens, however, are so delicious and baby beet greens, with a tiny beet on the end of them, are such a gourmet treat that you can hardly look upon harvesting them as a chore. With tiny seeds, like those of the lettuces, it is sometimes possible to avoid sowing too thickly if you mix the seeds first with sand.

TOPSOIL Topsoil is the first layer of soil on the earth. Often, as in urban gardens, it has either been stripped off and taken away to be sold, or turned over during construction so that it is buried underneath infertile subsoil. It takes about two hundred years to create topsoil, and it is an endangered natural resource; about five tons of topsoil are lost per acre per farm each year in just the United States alone. Chemical farming, which does not replenish the nutrients depleted by crops and destroys the soil's ability to enrich itself, is an important factor in this loss of soil fertility.

TRACE ELEMENTS Trace elements are mineral nutrients present in soil and plants in such minute quantities that we probably have not discovered all of them even today. The fact that they exist in tiny quantities, however, is not related to their importance; we have found that trace elements are just as essential to healthy life as nutrients found in large quantities.

Manure, compost, and humus will ensure that your soil has all the necessary trace elements, even though you garden intensively. Organic fertilizers naturally contain more trace elements than chemical fertilizers, especially those that are derived from petroleum.

Among the trace elements that we have discovered so far are boron, cobalt, copper, iron, manganese, and zinc.

VIABLE Viable, in gardening, refers to seeds that are alive and will germinate. Generally speaking, seeds will stay viable a couple of years, but do not discard older seeds without testing them; lotus seeds hundreds of years old have been germinated by archaeologists.

To test seeds for germination, place a few between dampened paper towels and cover with plastic. Check every so often to make sure no mold has developed and discard a batch if it has. Keep a record so you know the usual germination time, and then give the seeds a day or so more. You will know they are germinating when they send out tiny shoots.

WOOD ASHES If you have a wood stove or fireplace or know someone who does, you will have a good supply of wood ashes and should make use of them; they will save you money otherwise spent on fertilizers and are handy for many garden uses.

Wood ashes are alkaline and contain about 2 percent phosphorus and 1–10 percent potash, depending on what kind of wood they come from. They can be used alone or combined with other fertilizers, dug into the soil or used as a mulch. Wood ashes used as a mulch will deter cutworms and slugs as long as they are dry. Do not put the ashes too close to the stems of plants or over a newly sown seedbed; they are best used for side-dressing.

Once your plants are mature, dusting them with sifted ashes will act as a natural pesticide; do not spread thickly and do not use with acid-loving plants. If you notice any adverse leaf reaction, such as discoloring, do not use on that type of plant again.

Index